notes on love

Also by F.S. Yousaf

Euphoria

Sincerely

Serenity

Oaths

Prayers of My Youth

notes on love

poems and photography

F. S. YOUSAF

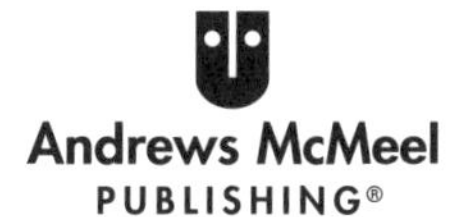

The authorised representative in the EEA is Simon and Schuster Netherlands BV, Herculesplein 96 3584 AA Utrecht, Netherlands. (info@simonandschuster.nl)

Andrews McMeel Publishing
a division of Andrews McMeel Universal
1130 Walnut Street, Kansas City, Missouri 64106

www.andrewsmcmeel.com

26 27 28 29 30 RLP 10 9 8 7 6 5 4 3 2 1

ISBN: 979-8-8816-0537-7

Library of Congress Control Number: Number on file.

Editor: Danys Mares
Art Director/Designer: Julie Barnes
Production Editor: Jennifer Straub
Production Manager: Julie Skalla
Proofreader: Faye Wikner
Film Scanned By: Taaha Siddiqui and Photo Life, Brooklyn

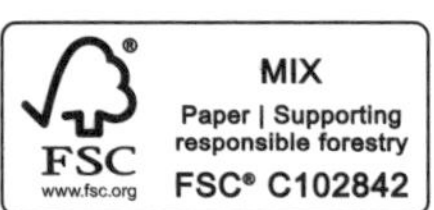

ATTENTION: SCHOOLS AND BUSINESSES
Andrews McMeel books are available at quantity discounts with bulk purchase for educational, business, or sales promotional use. For information, please email the Andrews McMeel Publishing Special Sales Department:
sales@andrewsmcmeel.com.

Dedicated to

Yusra, for always giving me reasons

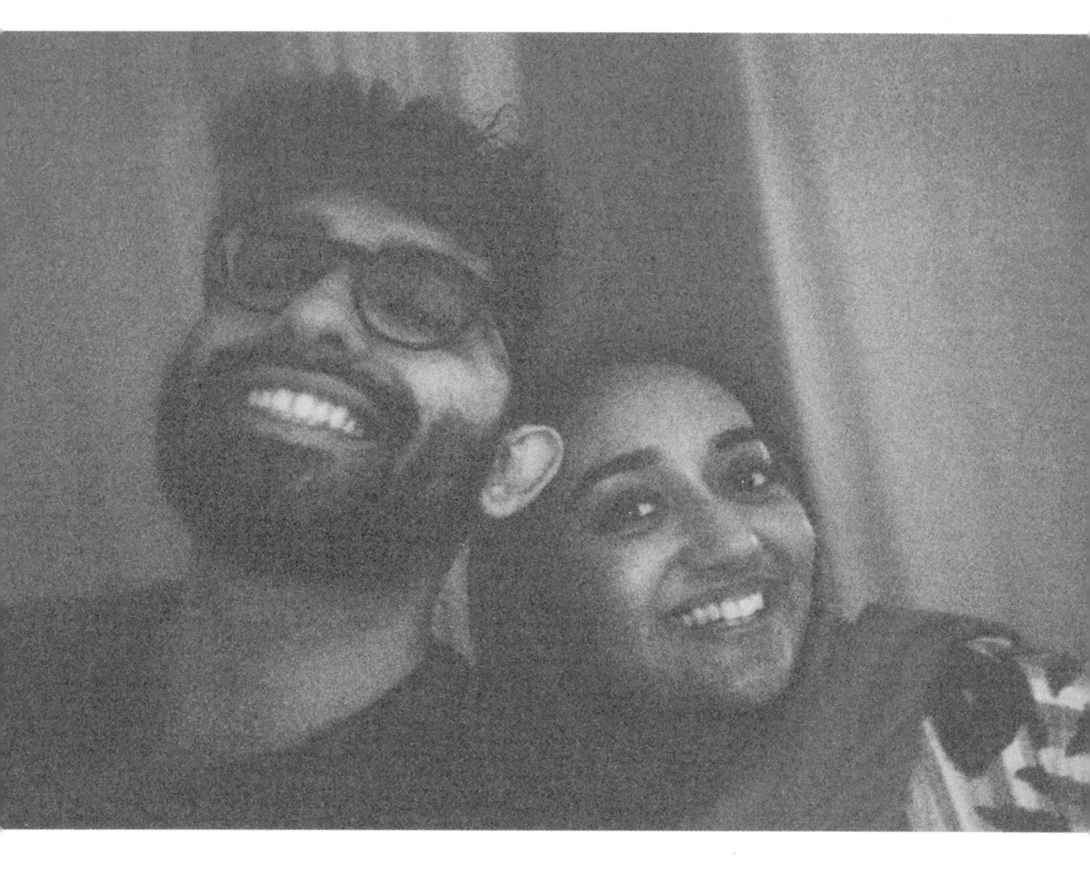

Dear Reader,

Ever since I started writing and got my first camera, I dreamed of this book coming to life. It's a project I set out to do back in 2018, before *Sincerely* was published.

In an attempt to be more present in everyday life, I started photographing quiet acts of love that I witnessed all around me. It gave me a new perspective on life to see how much love truly filled the world if we just took a second to look around, to take in those around us.

Along with these photographs, I have included poems on love, about love, and for love. Love is a topic I enjoy writing about, and I hope everyone who picks this book up can share in that enjoyment.

With love and gratitude,
FSY

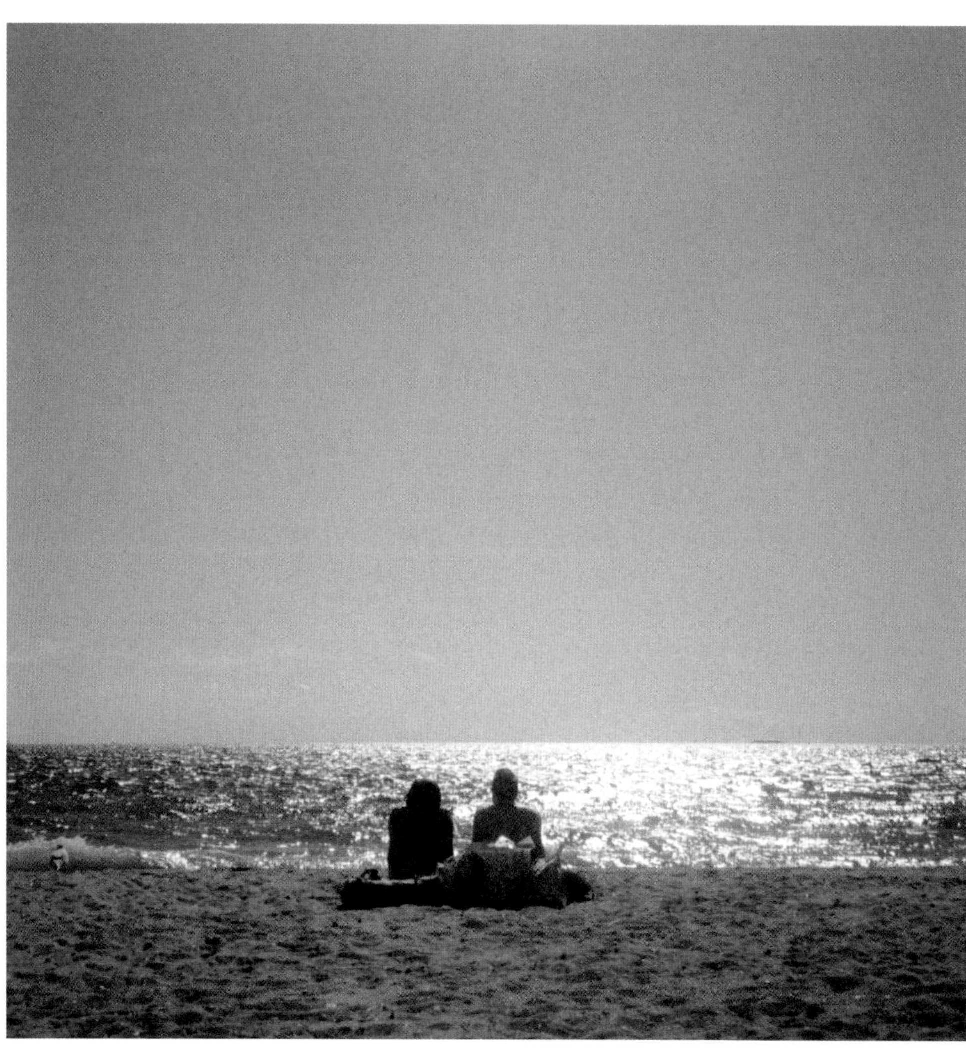

THAT WHICH BRINGS CALM

Laying in your lap
listening to the hymn of the sea.
All that is surrounding us, drowning away
until only we are left.

The oceans melody, as it performs
for its lone crowd, is not comparable
to any sound on this earth.

Its rhythm and tune,
the destructive force crashing down

encore after encore.

STILLNESS

We stand at the West 4th St subway station,
where the night chill has cooled off
the day's humidity. We're in the midst of
the ever-changing crowds and we hold
onto our cadence, our very own
quietude. Till the next train
screeches before us.

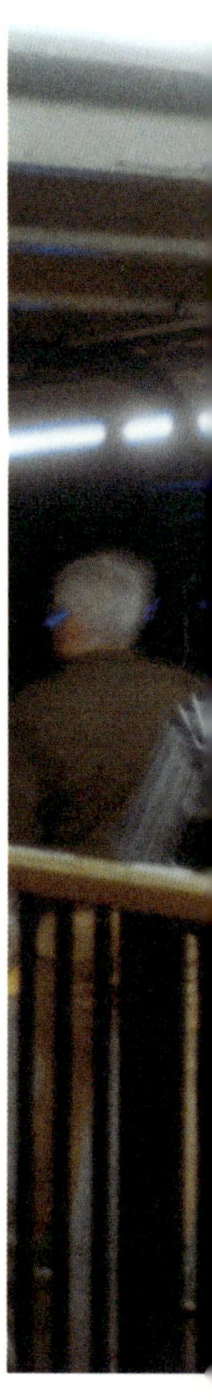

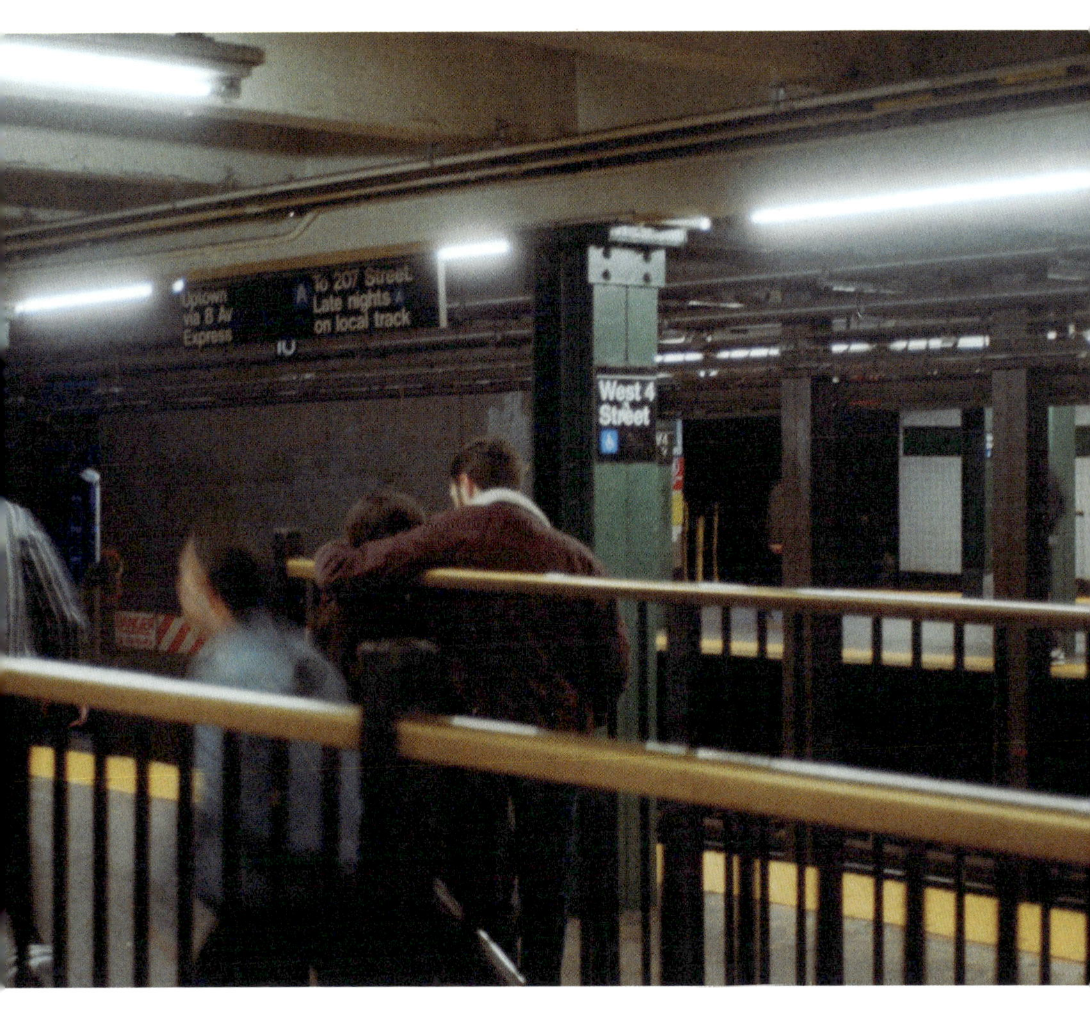
Uptown
via 8 Av
Express
To 207 Street
Late nights
on local track
West 4
Street

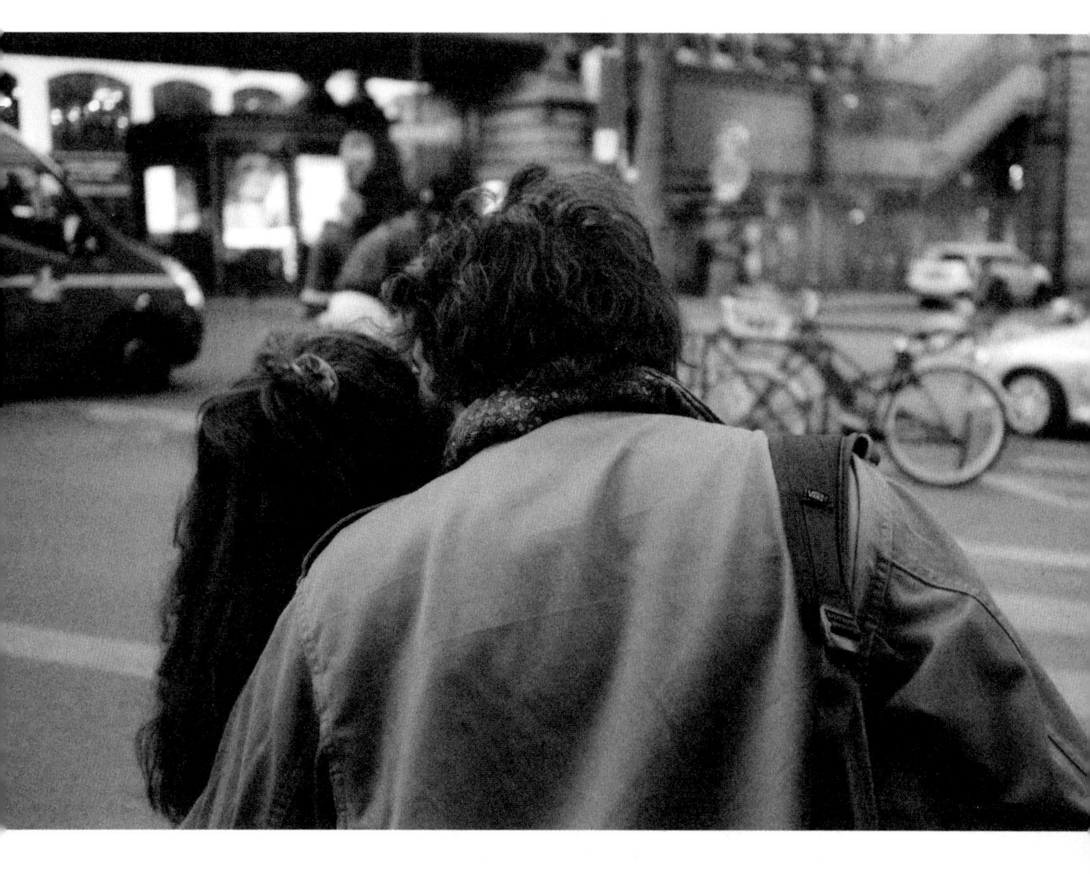

I ONLY ASK OF YOU
TO BECOME THE VERY BLESSING
I AM ABLE TO WORSHIP

YOUR BODY IS A CANVAS

I learn to trace
the indents on your skin—the scars
on your body have known you longer.
I think of the times we have lived
without one another.

You ask me to imagine we never met
and under the patter of my fingers
dancing on your skin,
all I can tell you is that   I can't.

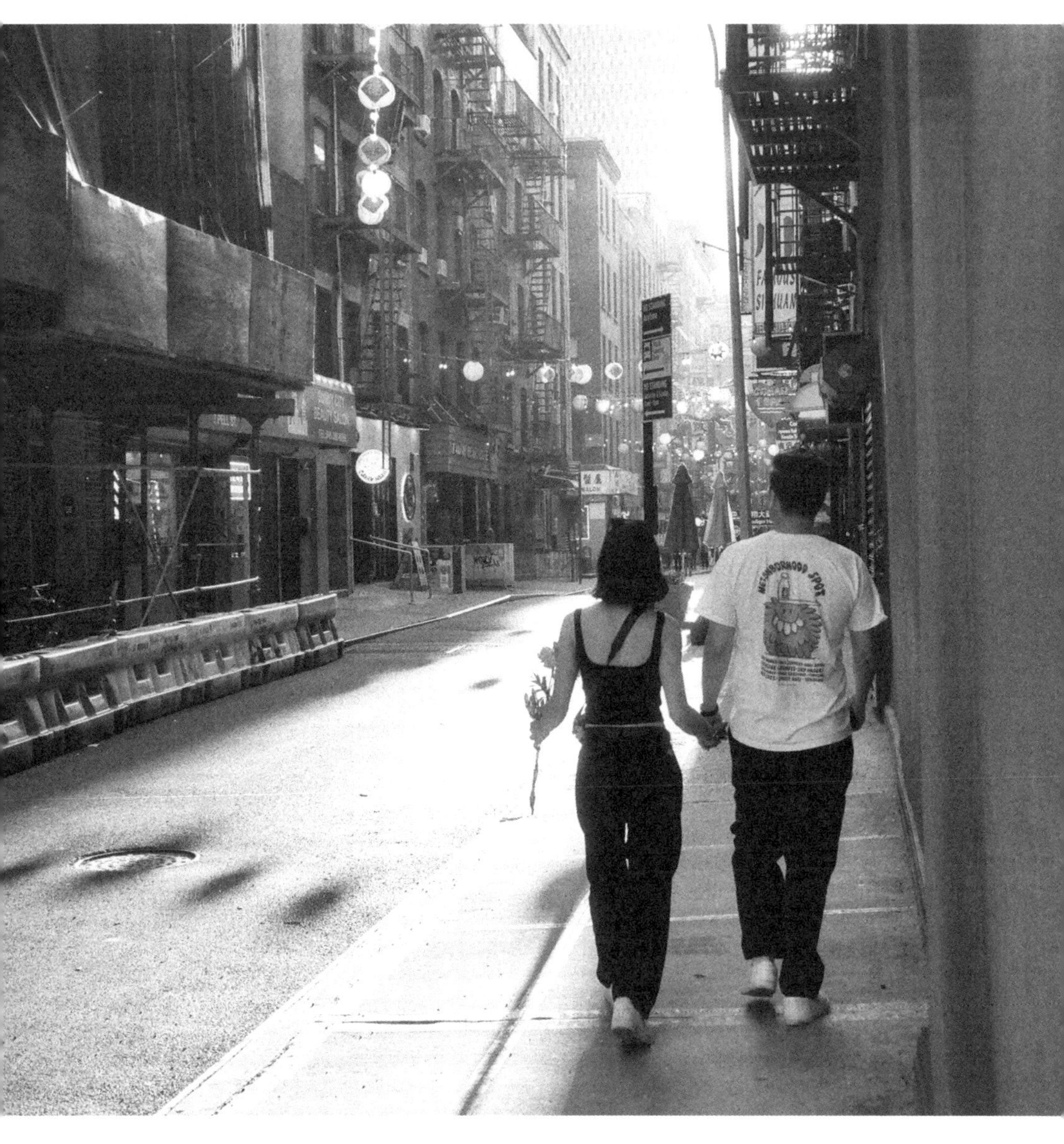

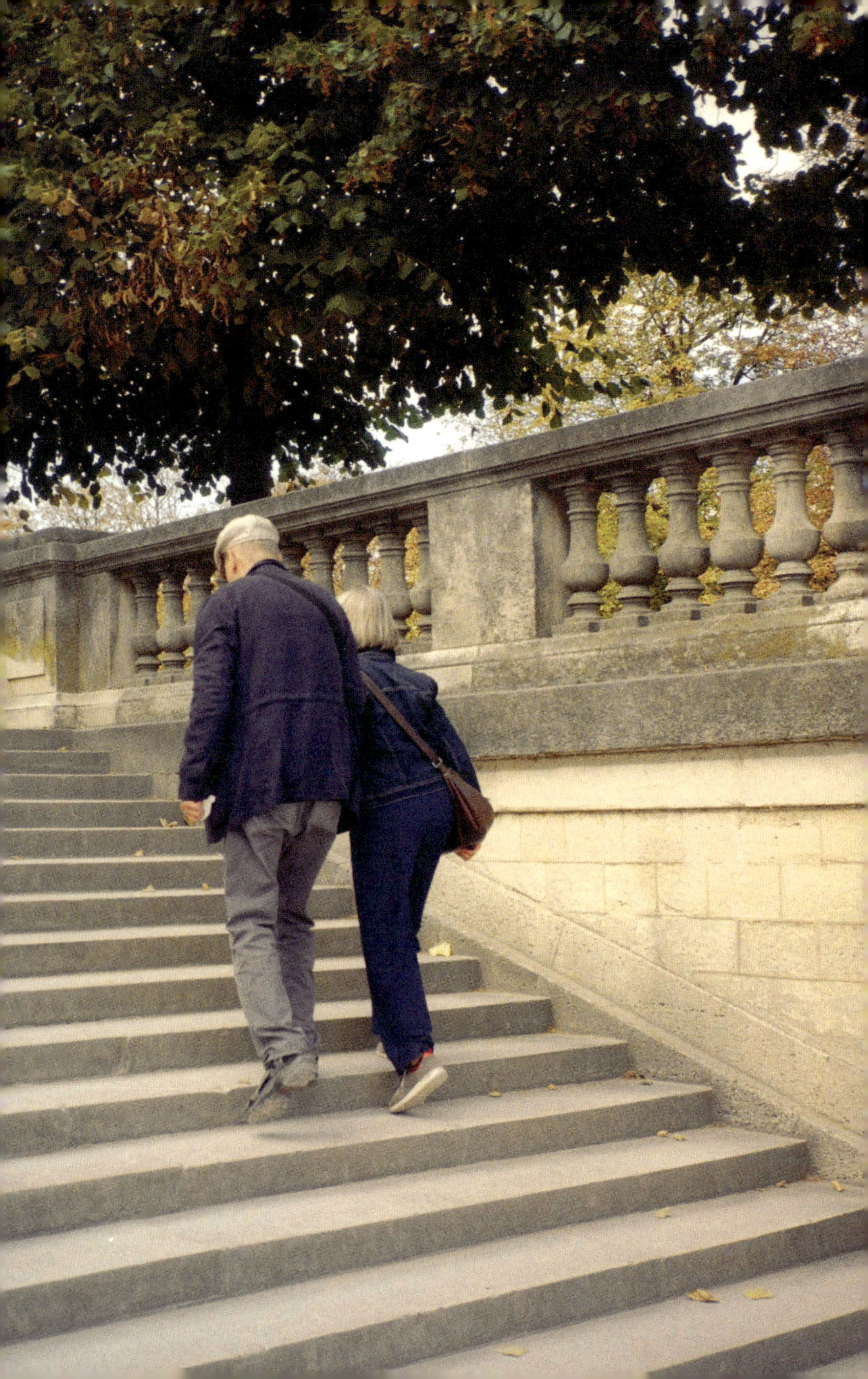

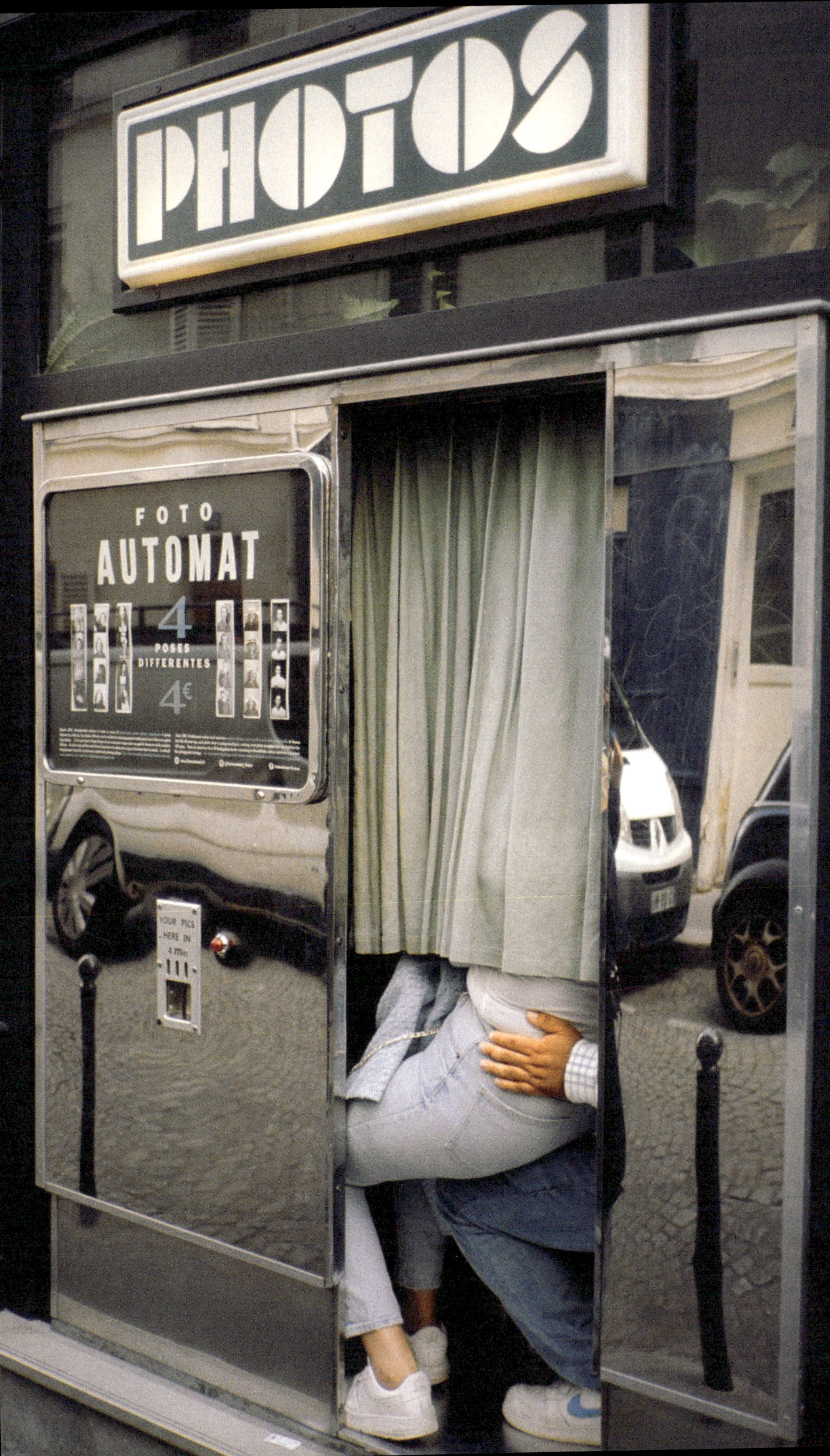
PHOTOS
FOTO
AUTOMAT
4
POSES
DIFFERENTES
4€
YOUR PICS
HERE IN
4 min

PARIS, 2023

Knot my fingers into yours. You brought me here,
don't you remember? Behind the wet-film photo booth
curtain, you sit in my lap after seeing
two before us do the same.

A woman with bright red lips
talking to those close. A cigarette tray.
I do not smoke, but I crave its scent.
Bland iced coffee, four slices
of buttered bread, a hot chocolate
half-empty, your shoulder against mine.

I have noticed that although we have seen this sun before,
it sets differently, weaving through buildings, the city
far off, and all around us living.

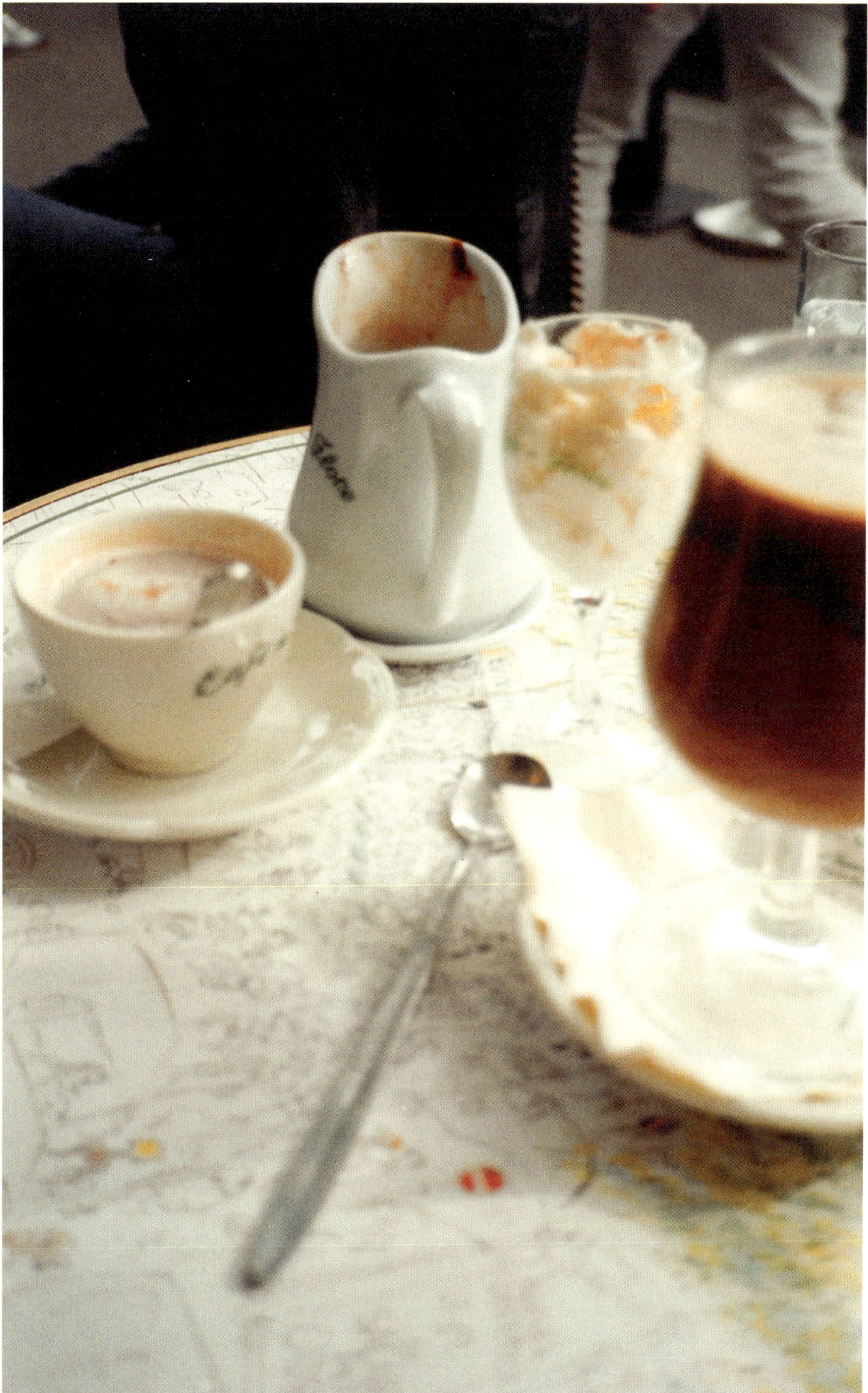

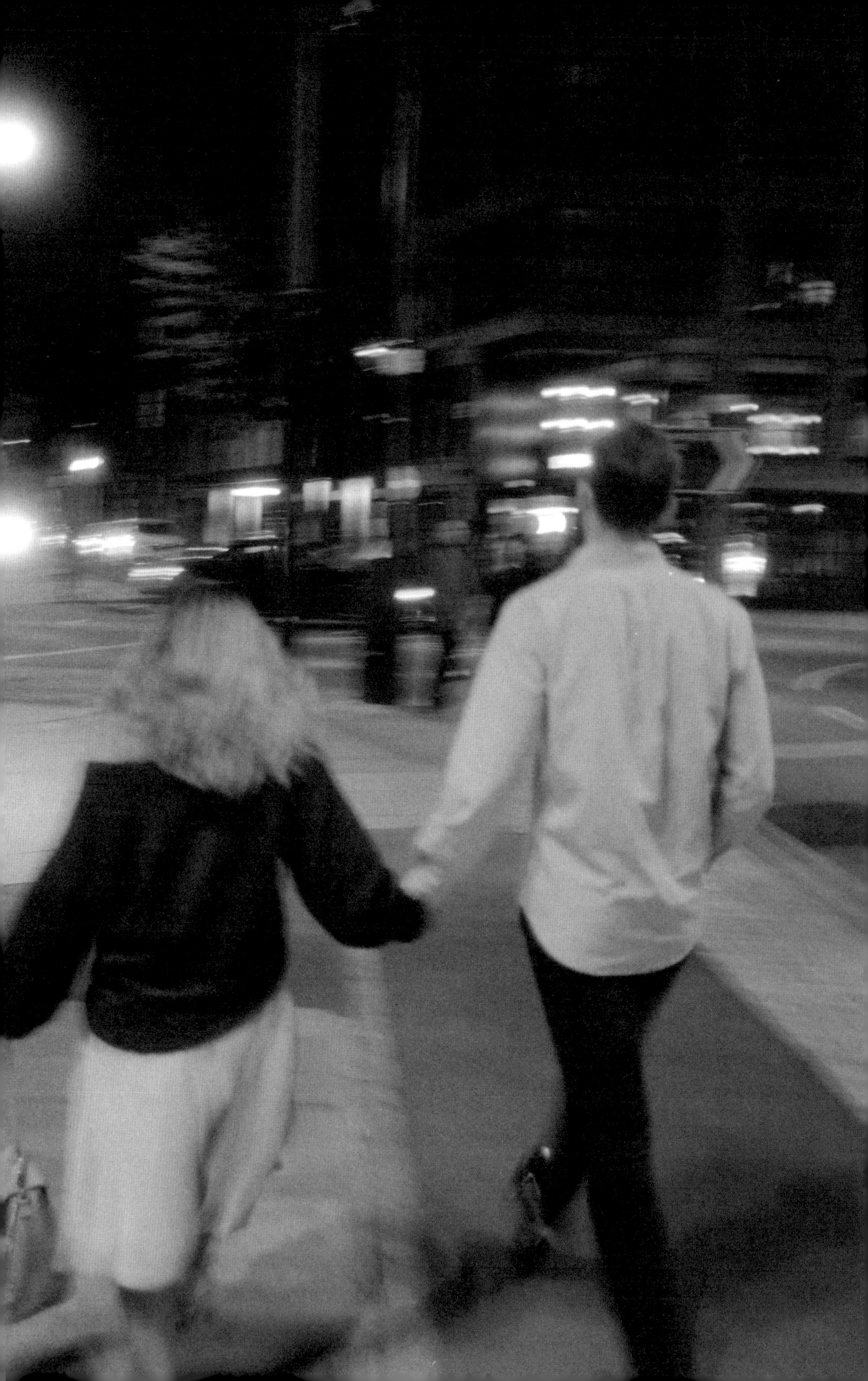

HERE IT WILL ALWAYS BE

Our shoes lay by the door,
under the soft instrumental music the record plays . . .
a whisper; at first, indecipherable.
But as your lips crease, I read your words
as if they are a novel made only for me, only me.

You cusp my hands, peel them off my cheeks
and hold them against yours.
Warmth—our skin intertwining.

You tell me the world rests nowhere else.

WITH EASE, WITH CALM

I feel your warm
exhale wrap around my skin,
and I'm shocked by how easily
my body disarms itself,
acknowledging all of my havens
before my mind
accepts it.

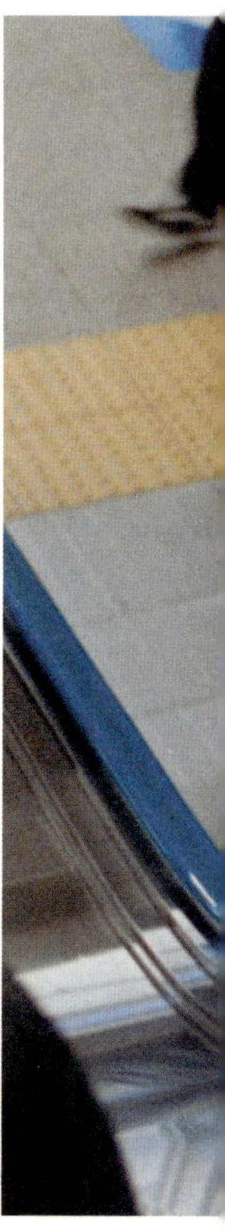

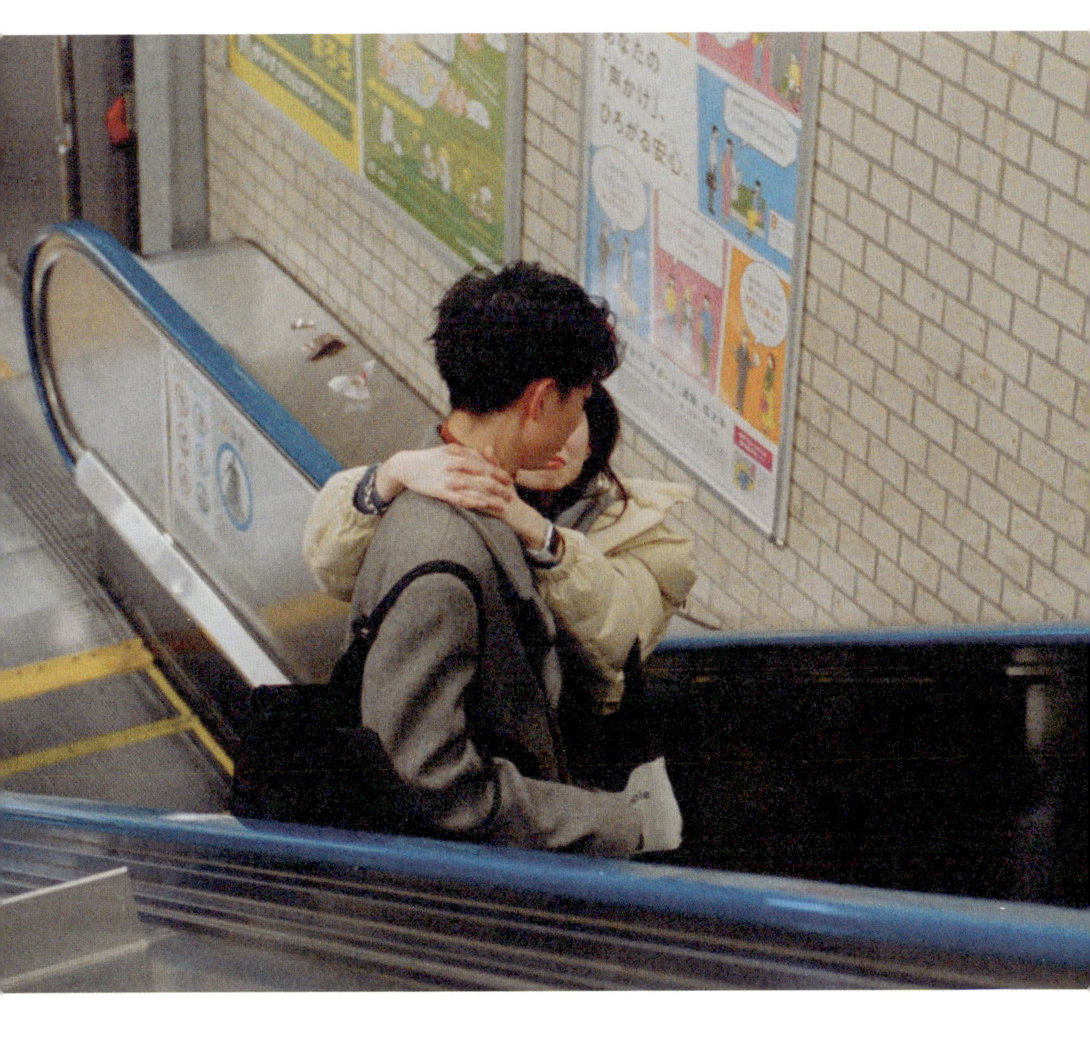
「声かけ」、
ひろがる安心。

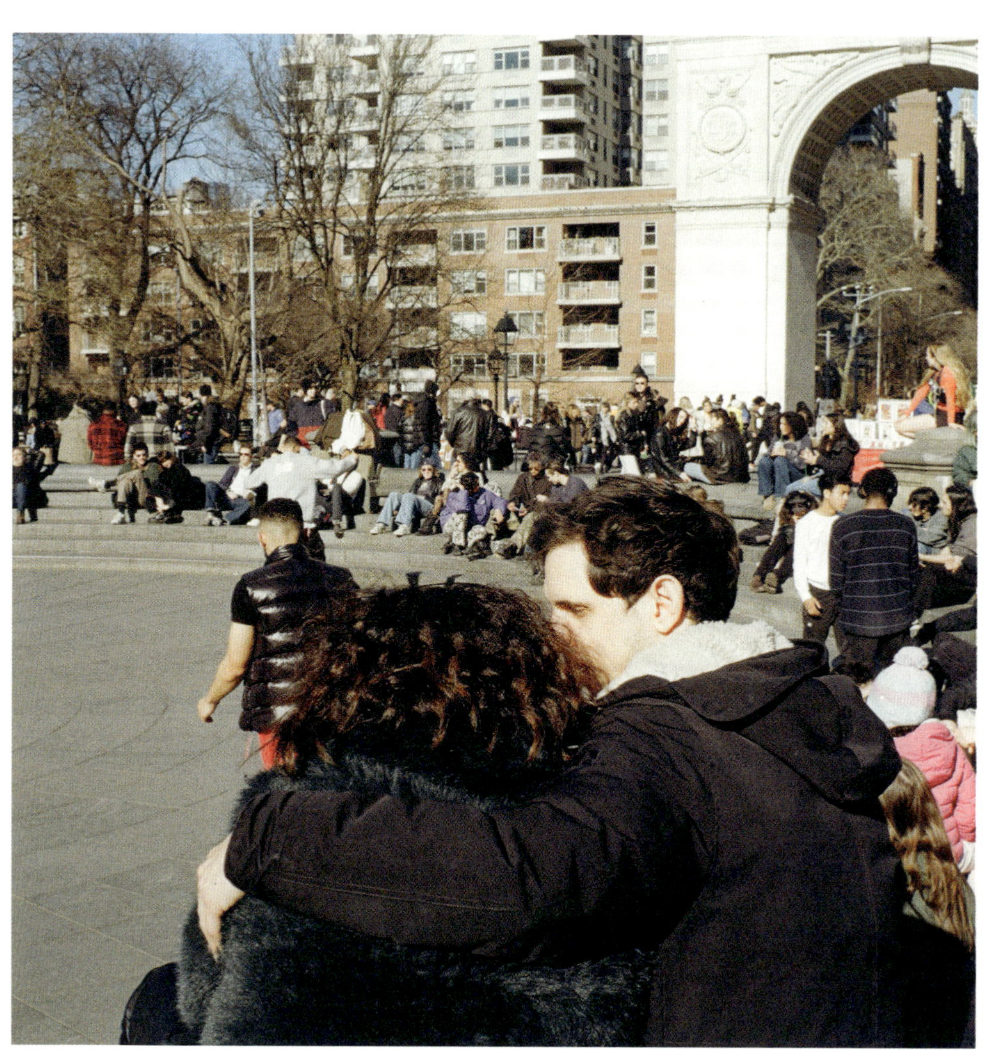

YOUR EYES ONLY

In all my years of living,
not many have known
the range of colors my name
can be. Yet, the desire
to be recognized fades
in your presence.

ON THE TRAIN BACK HOME

Her head resting on my shoulder, as if god had carved my body for her to gather herself into. The pop of our ears, exiting the pure black tunnel into the cloudy night sky. I remember how quiet her voice sounded when she told me she enjoyed our little life. My earbuds stay in my pocket—I want her life echoing off my skin. All I desire is the irrevocable normalcy of a simple life.

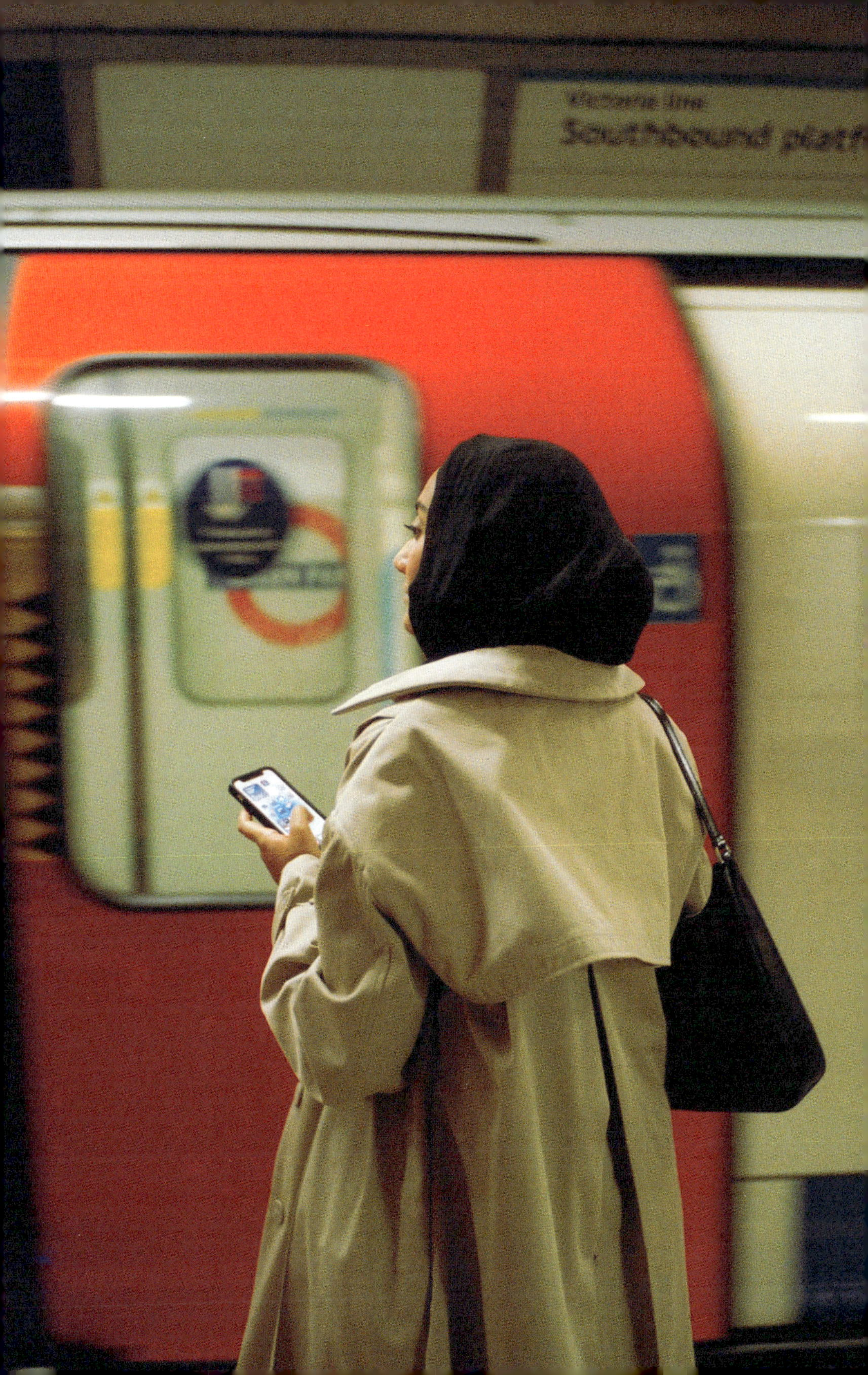
Southbound

I find the meaning
of life in the crease of the soft
wrinkle on your palm

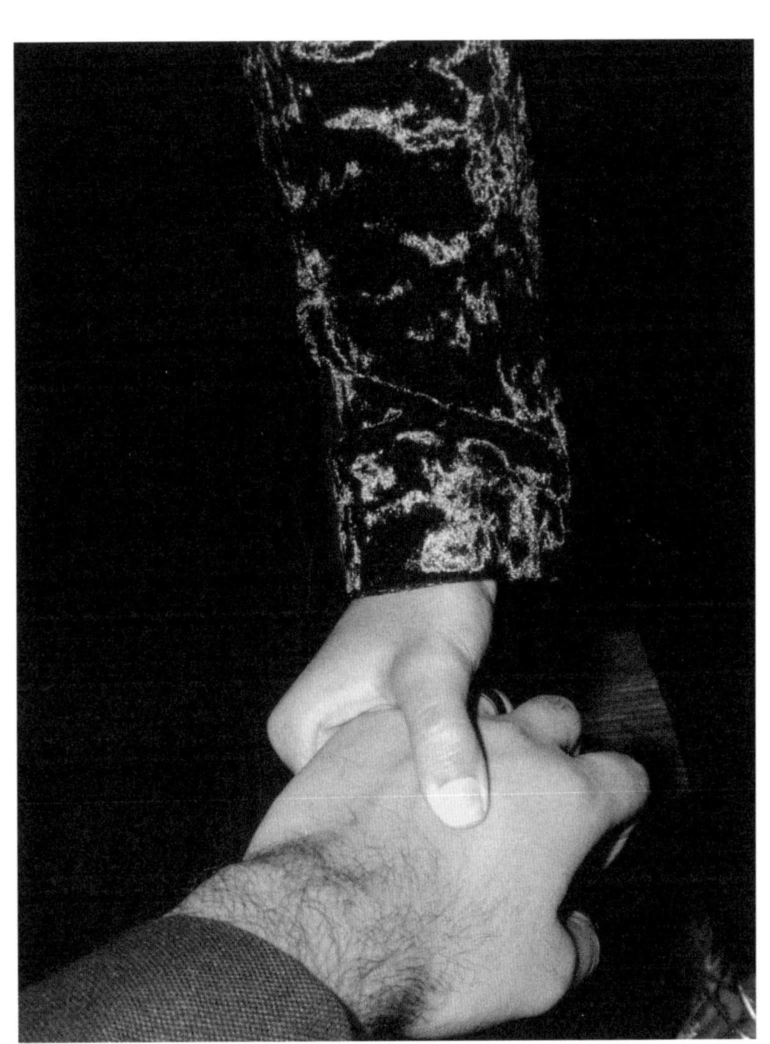

BALLADS

The echo of your voice,
tuned like an instrument—a choir
of symphonies.

In the many sounds love holds,
I enjoy yours most.

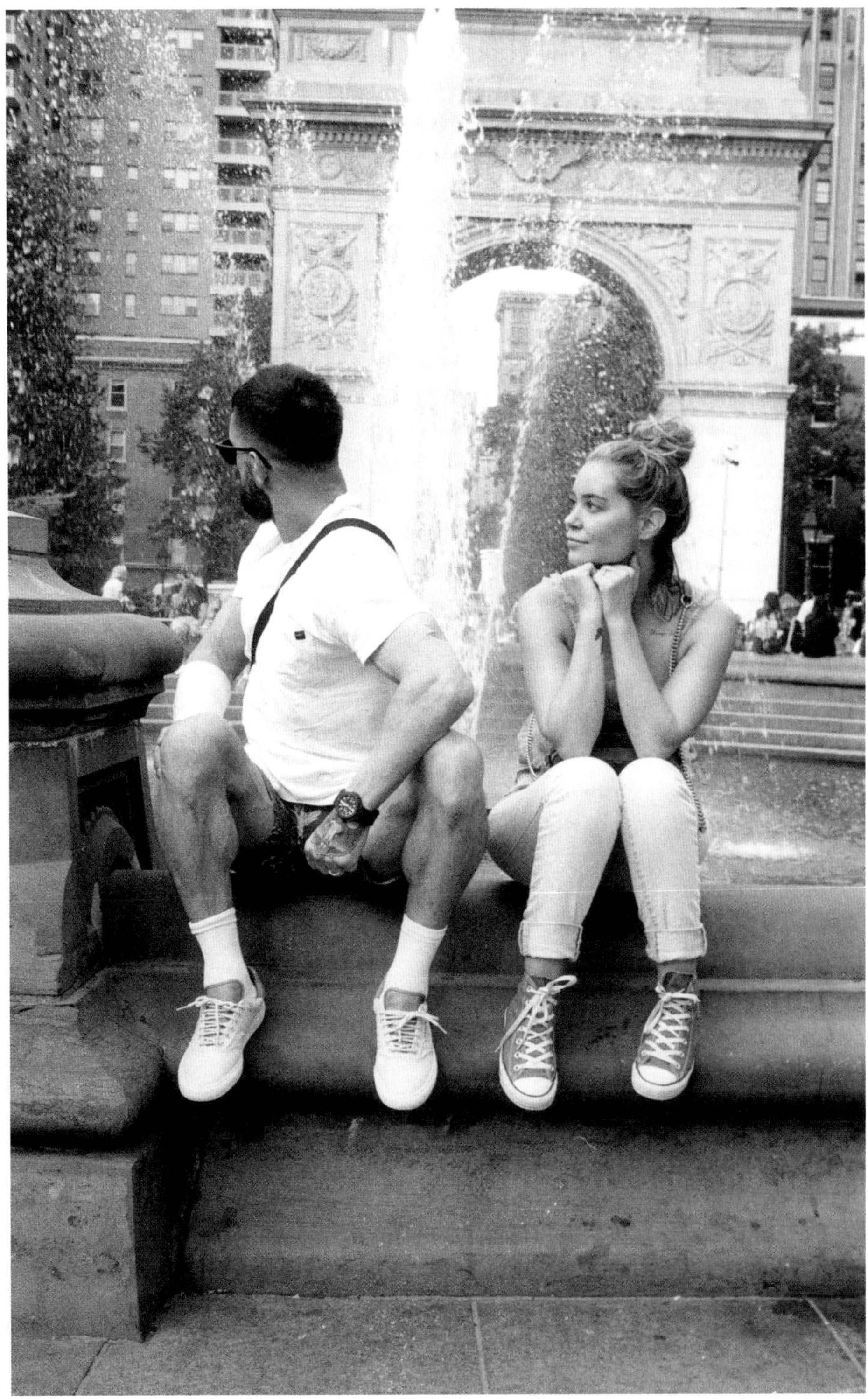

YOUR HAND REACHING FOR ME

Your hand subtly reaching for mine, holding me tightly as my life is dimming. When the past is creeping behind me so hungrily, I can't help but collapse into myself like a star. The remnants of those emotions endure, more real now than before. Behind the hopelessness, your hand remains, ensuring I can journey back to the present in one piece.

I HOLD ON TIGHT

With your hands in mine, I closed
my eyes. Fear, for once, taking
on a different shape, easier to grasp.
I take it in, acceptance of merely this. This.

IN THE CORNER OF THE PARK

Under orange skies, I've found patience.
Have you heard me over the
chatter on the bridge? I speak for only you.
Let the others hear—it doesn't bother me
anymore.

I still think of the tree in Central Park
where we shared our first kiss.
Often, I wander toward it, the only thought on my mind
of how vast we've become. How age has dissolved
into numbers. We forget the passing years.
I still think back to us, long ago.
Children, smitten. Intoxicated with one another.
Who else has shared themselves here?

In this extension we've created, I cannot find myself
filling space with anything but you.

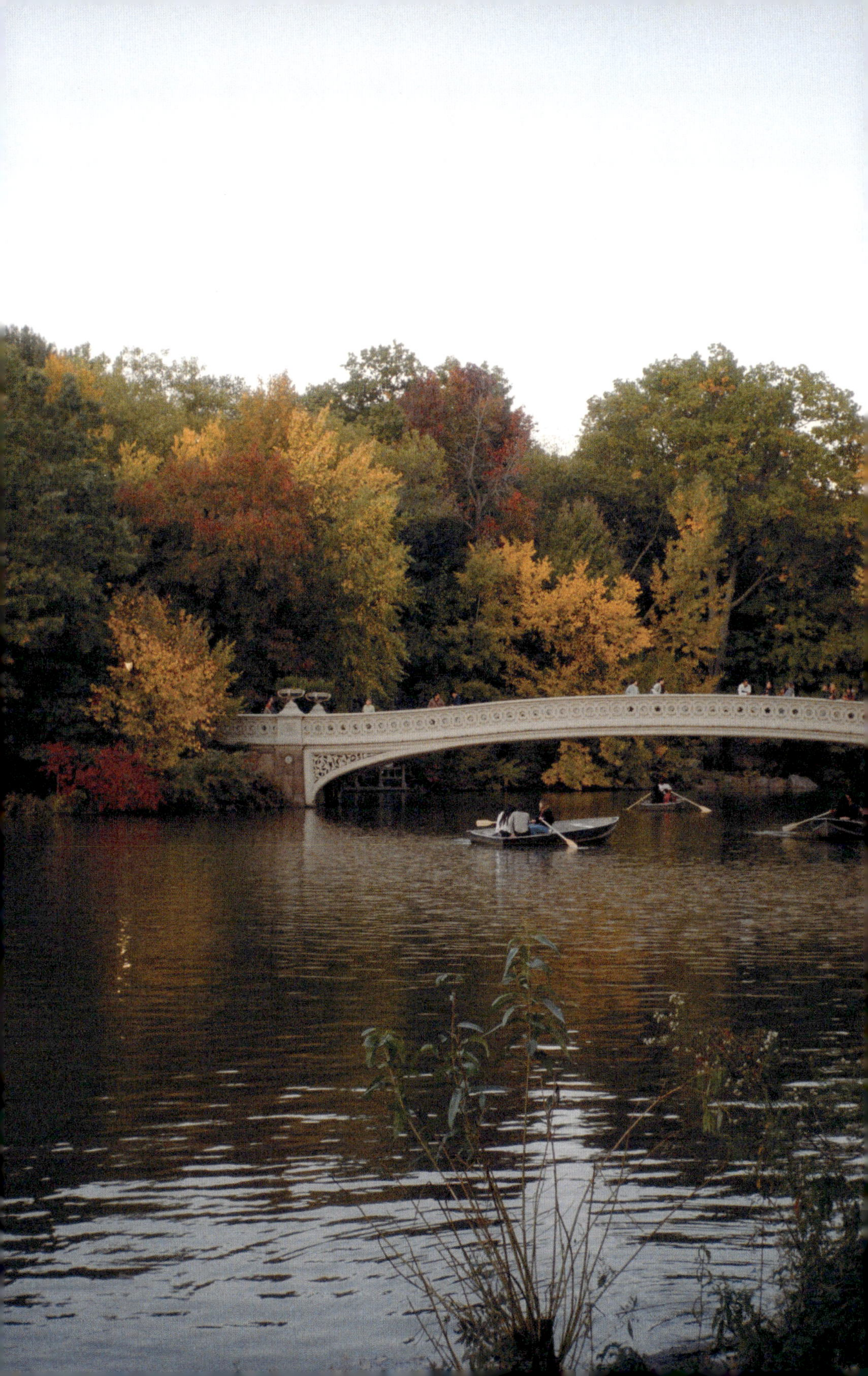

HOW CAN I POSSIBLY DESERVE YOUR LOVE WHEN I STRUGGLE TO SEE ALL THE GOOD YOU'VE SEEN IN ME?

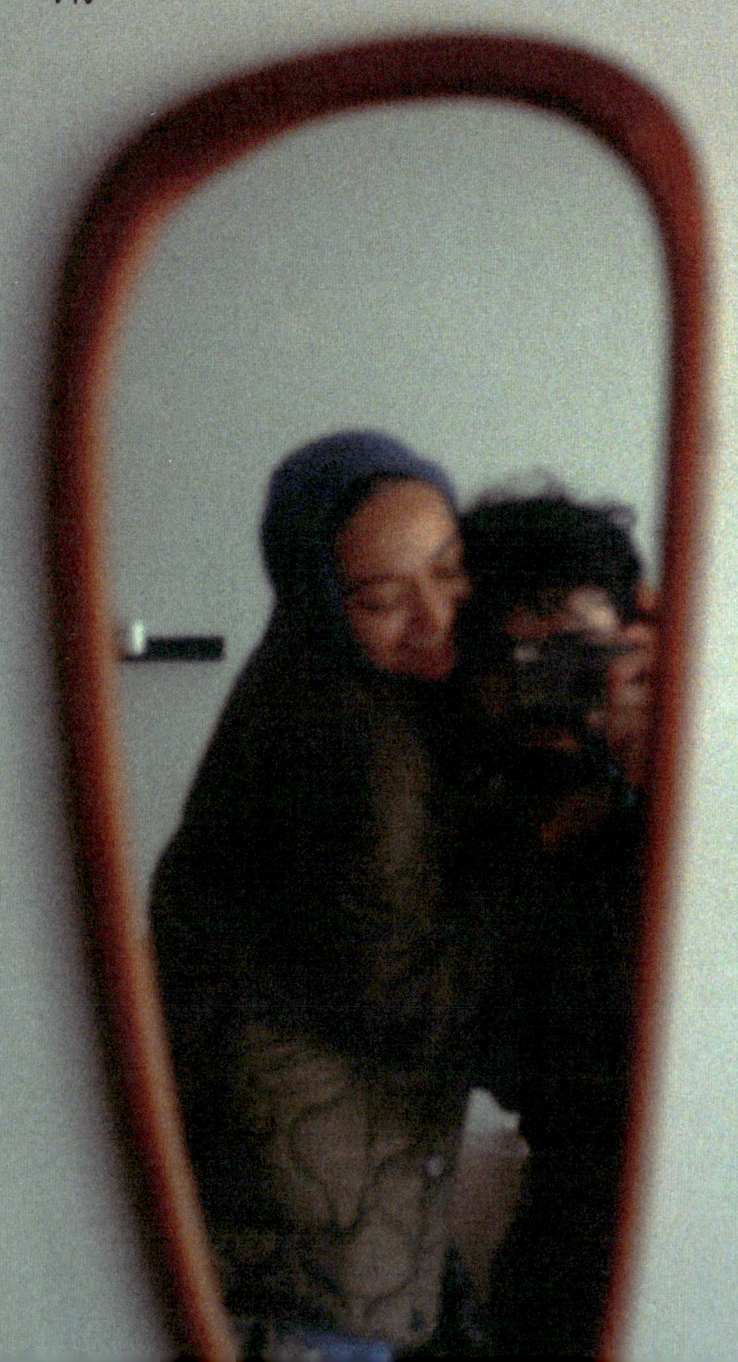

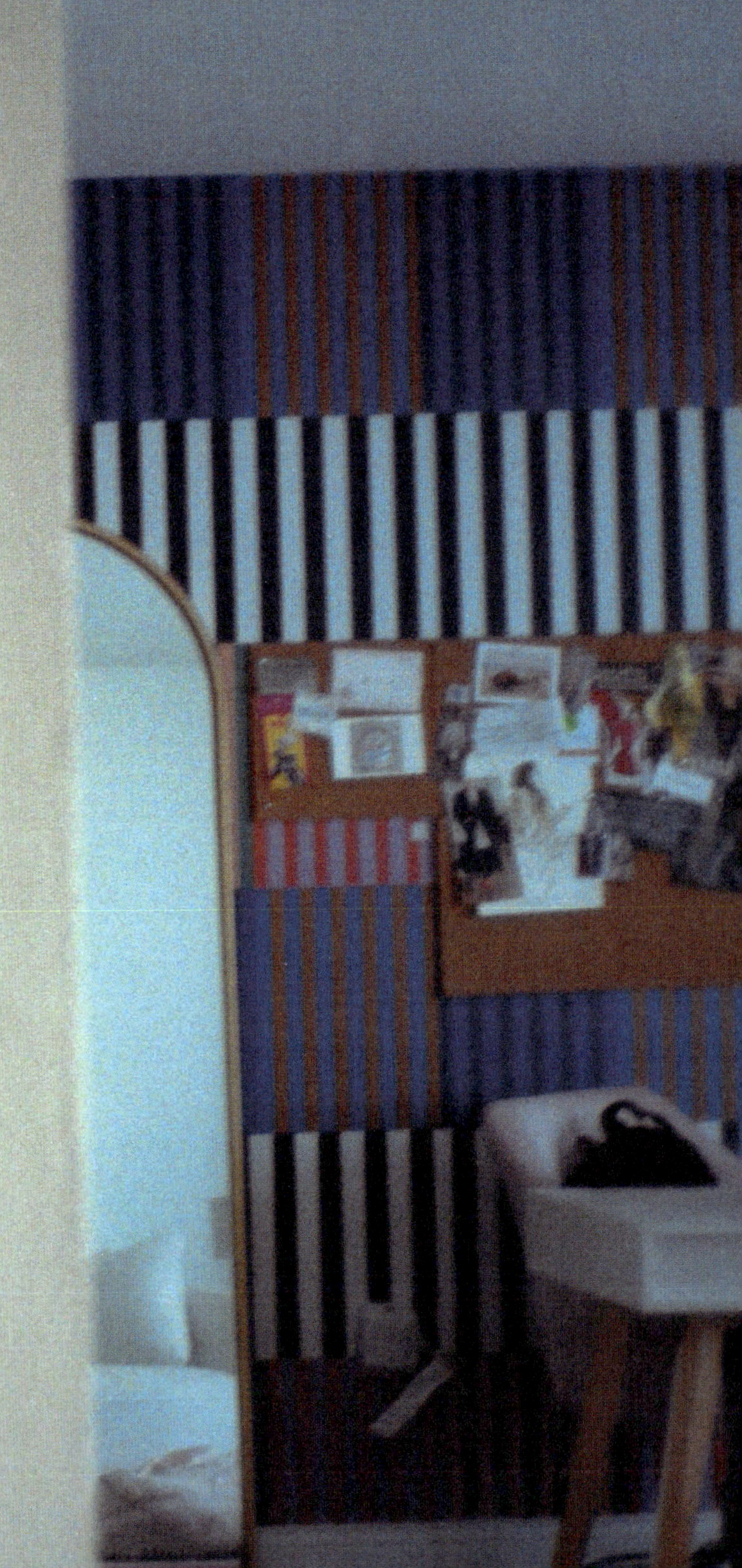

WE LIGHT EACH OTHER

I want you to know that
even when you think you're not
deserving of love,
I will find ways to illuminate you.

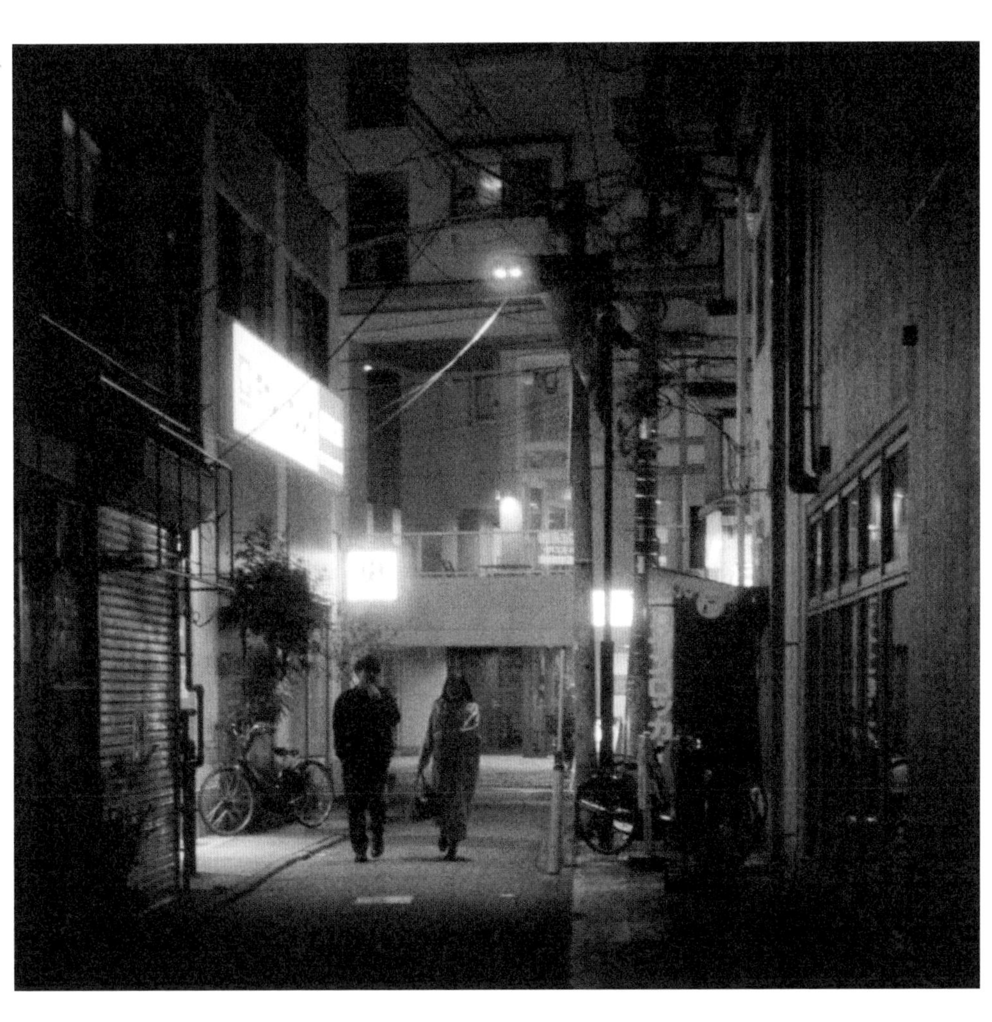

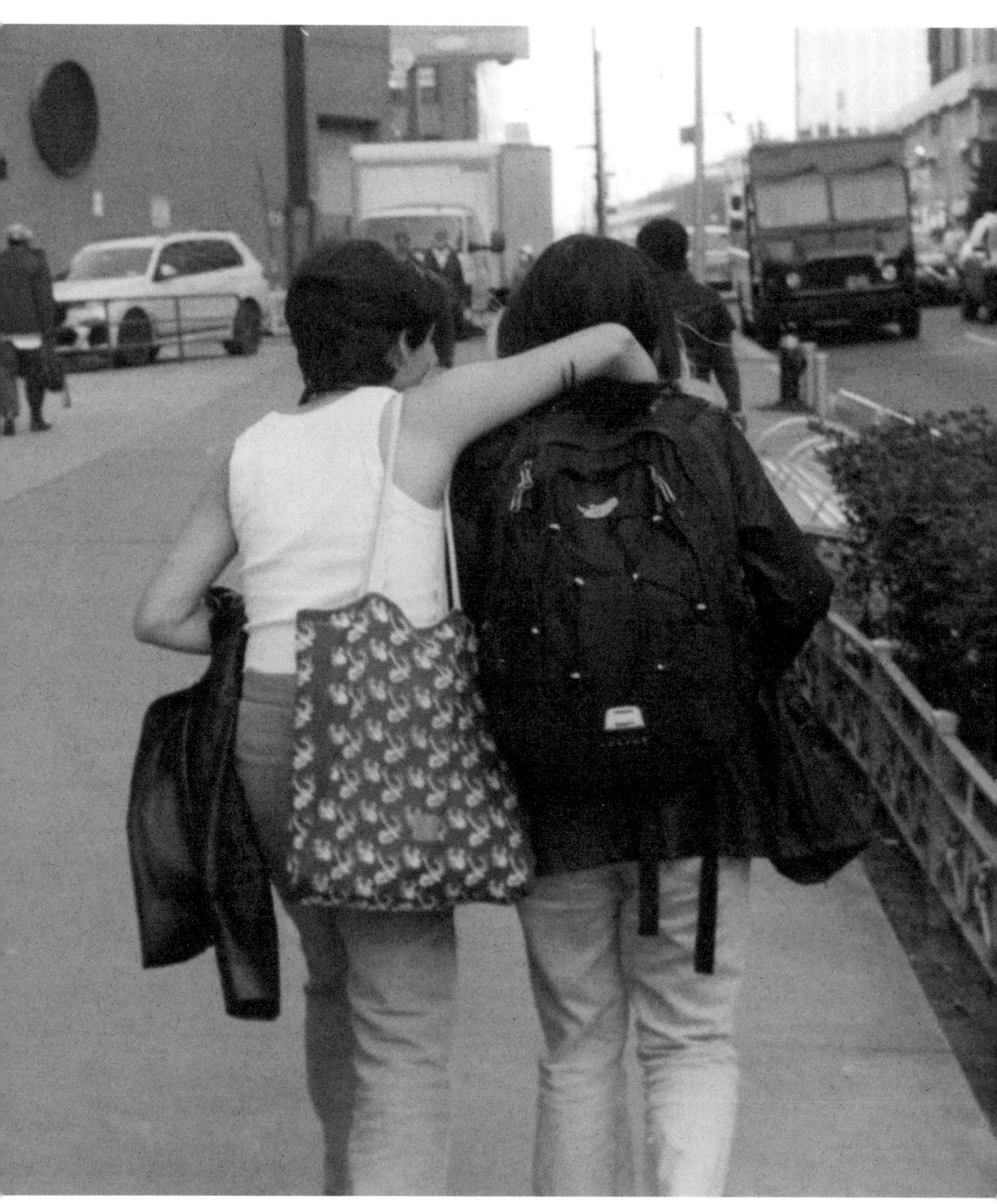

UNFOLD AND FLOURISH

I think of evolution often.
How your laugh comes easier
than years before.
Your eyes glisten differently but with the same
adoration as the first day I met you.

I find myself missing who you once were
but excited for the many ways
you will unfold as life flourishes.

AN ETERNITY

When I tell you that you make me feel infinite
I mean you make days never-ending.
The sun always shines on us, a breeze accompanying it.

I imagine myself as a child. Drifting
through large fields,
wondering what is next. Good or bad,
I overwhelm myself with the outcomes. But

with you, I close my eyes.
For whatever comes, we have eternity
to live on.

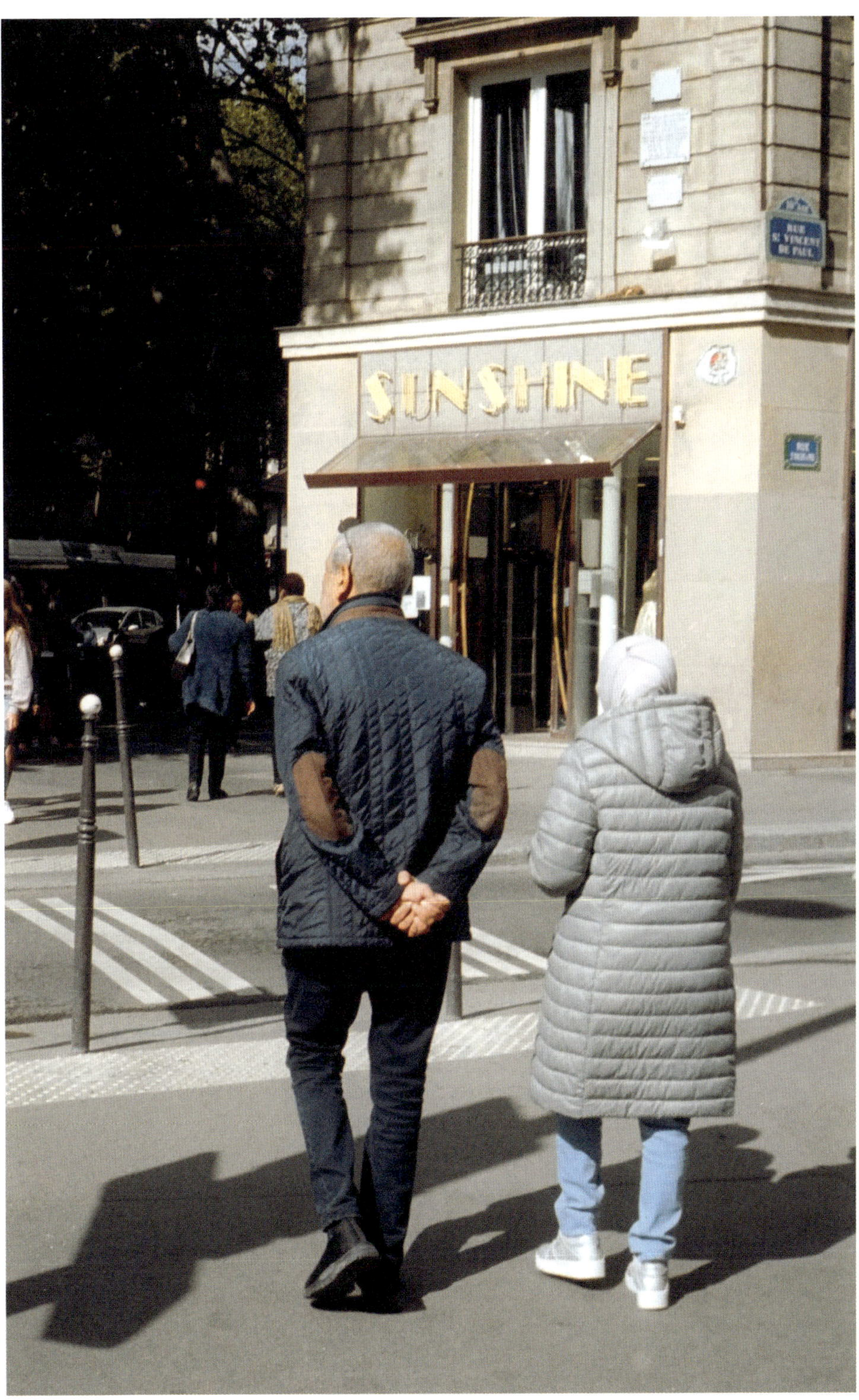
SUNSHINE

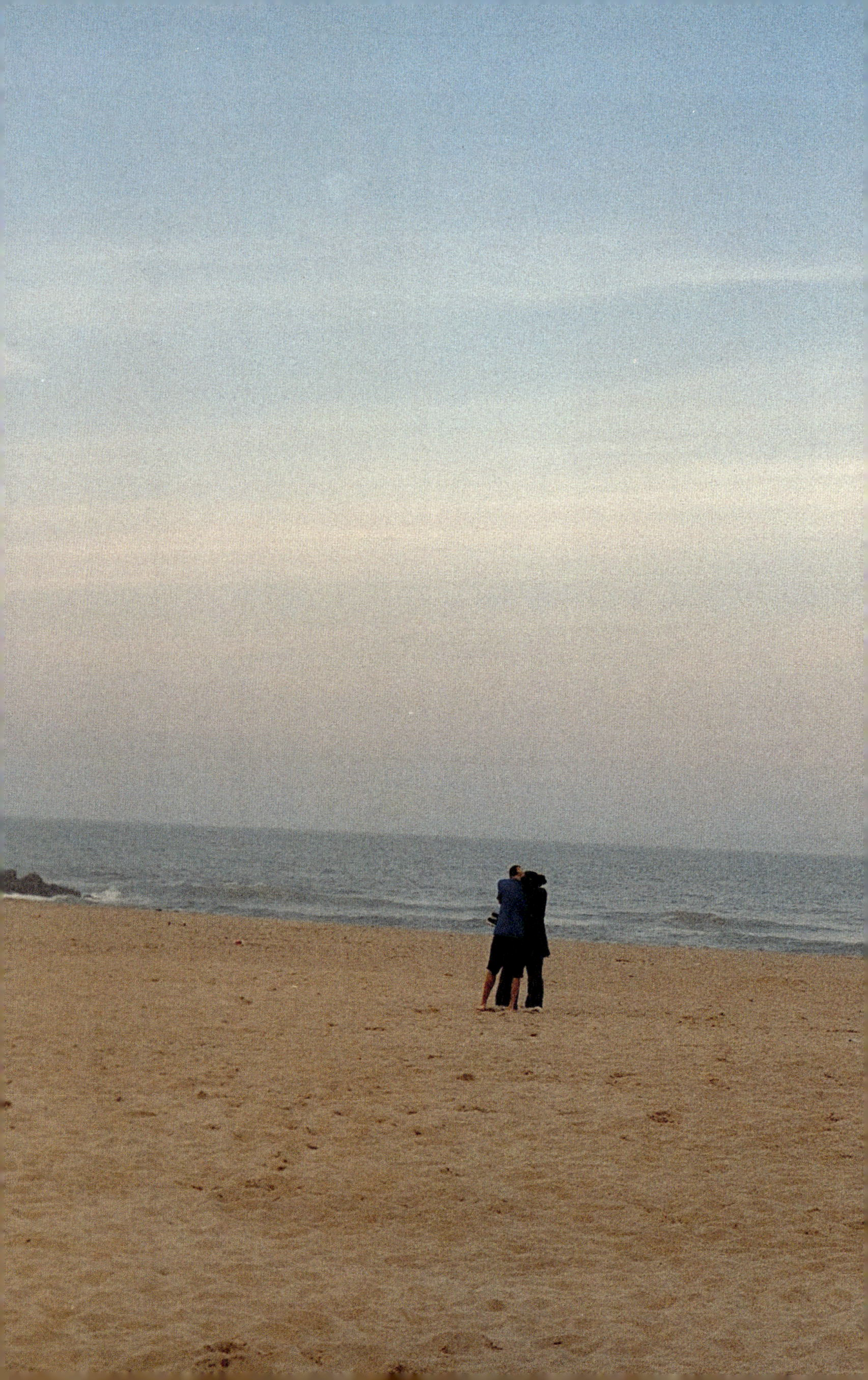

I HAVE EARS FOR YOU, ONLY YOU

We look at the ocean, watching others
swim. You hold a smooth shell

to your ear and tell me
the ocean calls

you. You gently hold
the shell up to my ears. I don't hear

an ocean, I hear your voice,
echoing pleasantly, as if it were waves

blanketing me.

SAY IT AGAIN, SO I REMEMBER LONGER

Sunflower petals rest
on the table. You call my name
through the bedroom door and
I can hear you clearly, yet
pretend your voice does not

reach me. So you must
say my name again—
with a
pang of impatience.

I brush the fallen
petals onto my palms.
I open the door.

Farhan ♡

DECEMBER STILLNESS

Dust gathers on our skin. You trace
your fingers on me like a windshield
on a snow-felled day.

A blurred self-portrait,
your heart, our initials.

When do you think these
specks will fall off us, if this
snow decides to melt?

TILL THE WITHERINGS

Our conversations come alive
when the air is crisp, the fan blowing,
despite snow piles outside the
windowsill. Both of us under the same blanket.
A soft tone caresses me—how you want our life to sprout
from here. *Water it,* you say. *Don't let it wither.*

The snow sticks to the window. I tell you
that I want to live as long as the gardens remain
in bloom.

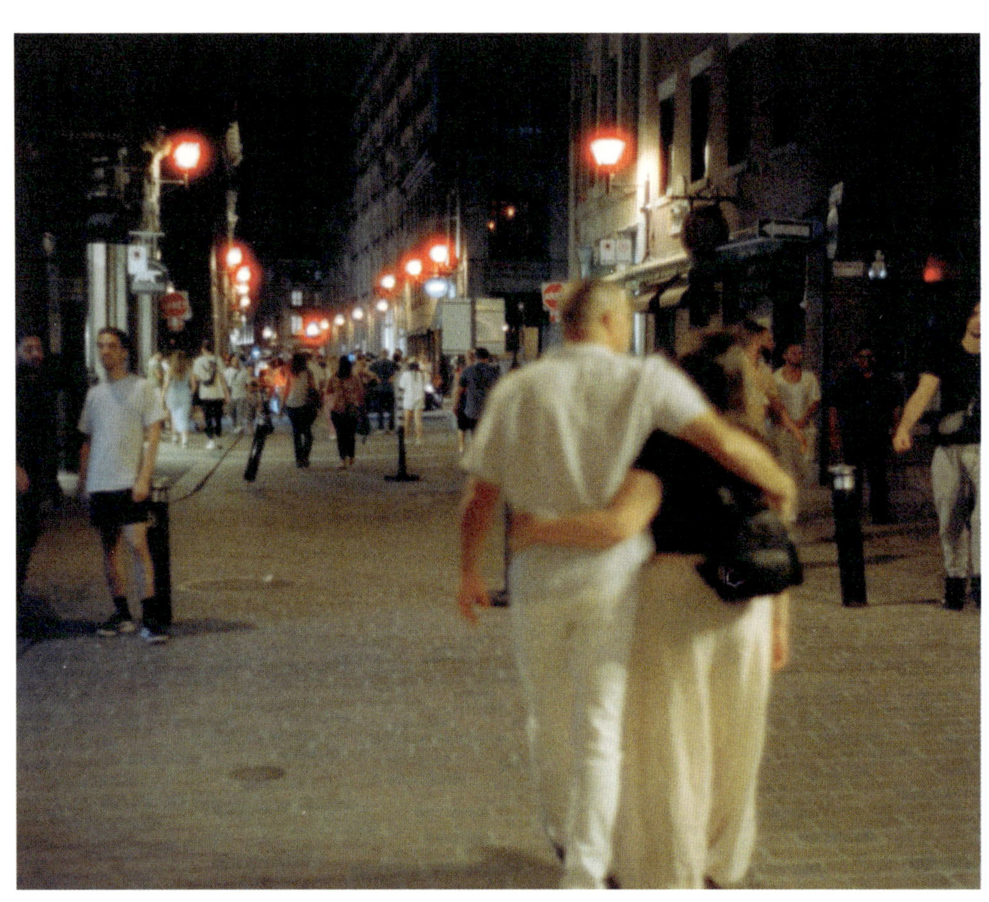

ALL OF ME, LOVED

It's an odd feeling—
being loved despite my flaws.
Almost as if they're accepted even
when I struggle saying my own name.

You tell me that the parts you love the most
about me are the ones I've been told
I need to despise.

That you embrace all of me.

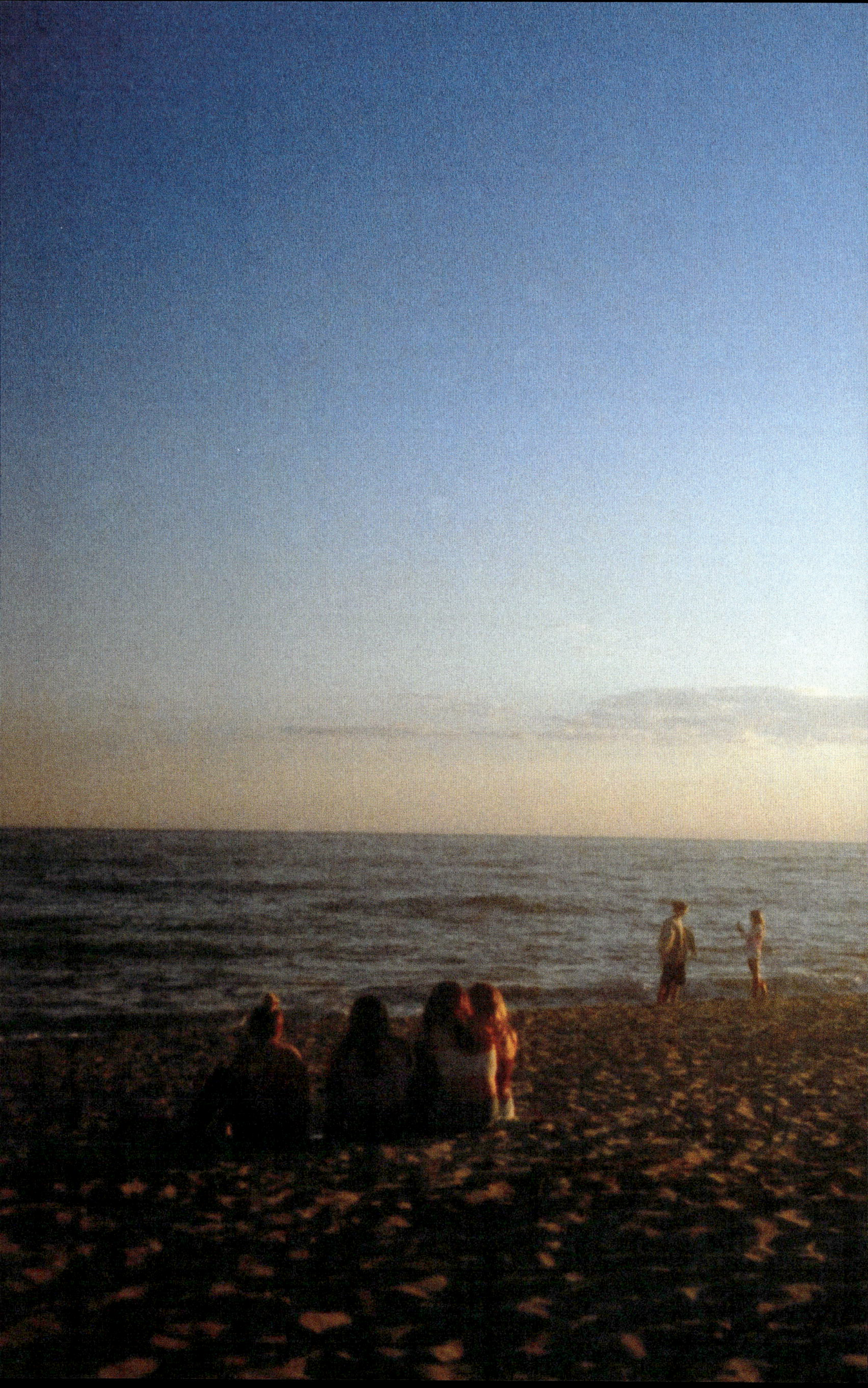

THIS WORLD IS OVERFLOWING WITH TENDERNESS— WE SIMPLY NEED TO OPEN OUR EYES AND SEARCH FOR IT.

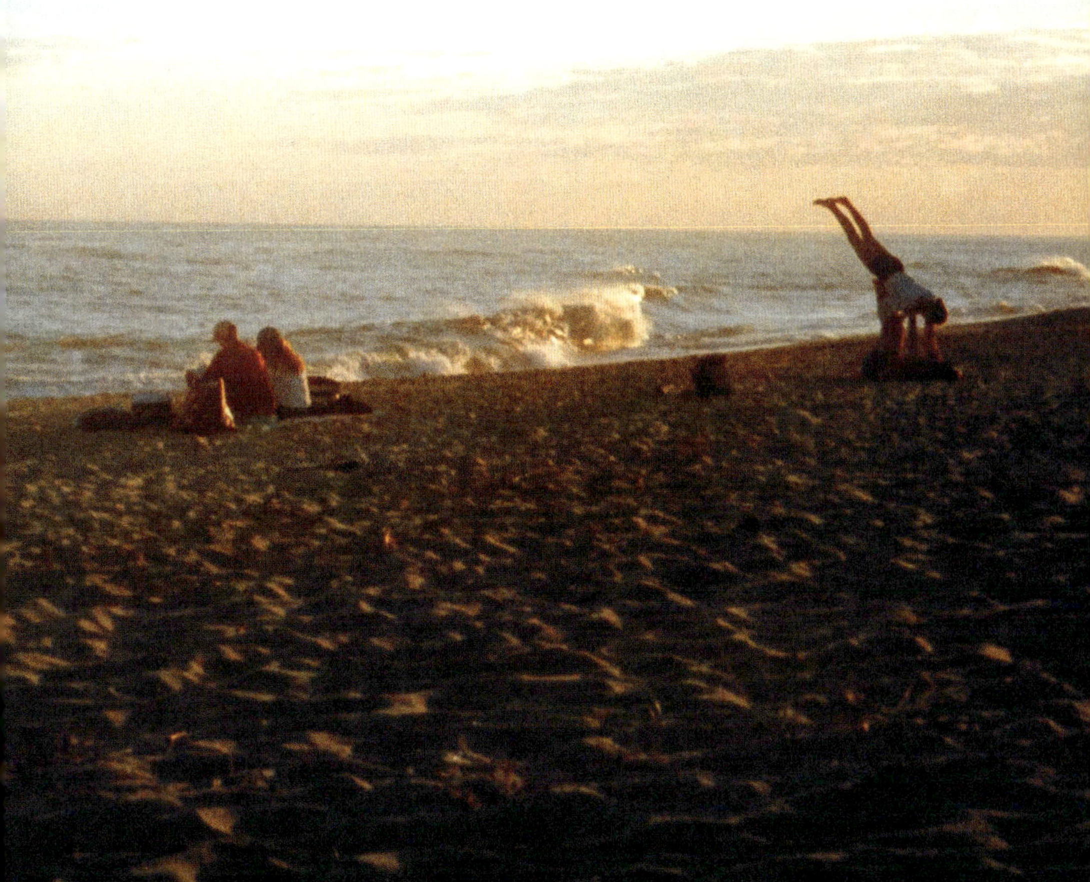

POCONOS, 2021

At the end of May, steam rose from the ground, yet the air was frigid. Our bones were stiff from the car ride, popping the trunk and unloading our bags into the brown oak cabin. There were five of us, each one I've grown up with as if we were planted in the same garden. We all understand each other's roots, especially in the years we grew in different directions in an effort to unearth more of ourselves. I think, more than must be good for me, about how only being surrounded with sisters has molded me. How my father left before I learned how to shave. The way I used to stay up past midnight to see my mother. Am I less of a man? Or more? Does it really matter? Because right now I am bound to those around me. I've placed my life in their palms, and they've tucked it in their pockets with their wallets and keys. I adore them and they adore me, and we'll never speak of it, but we'll know. After dinner with the sun setting, we take out board games and set them on the dining table, and we play even after the sun meets us again. I lose every game, laughing as we reset the board and play again.

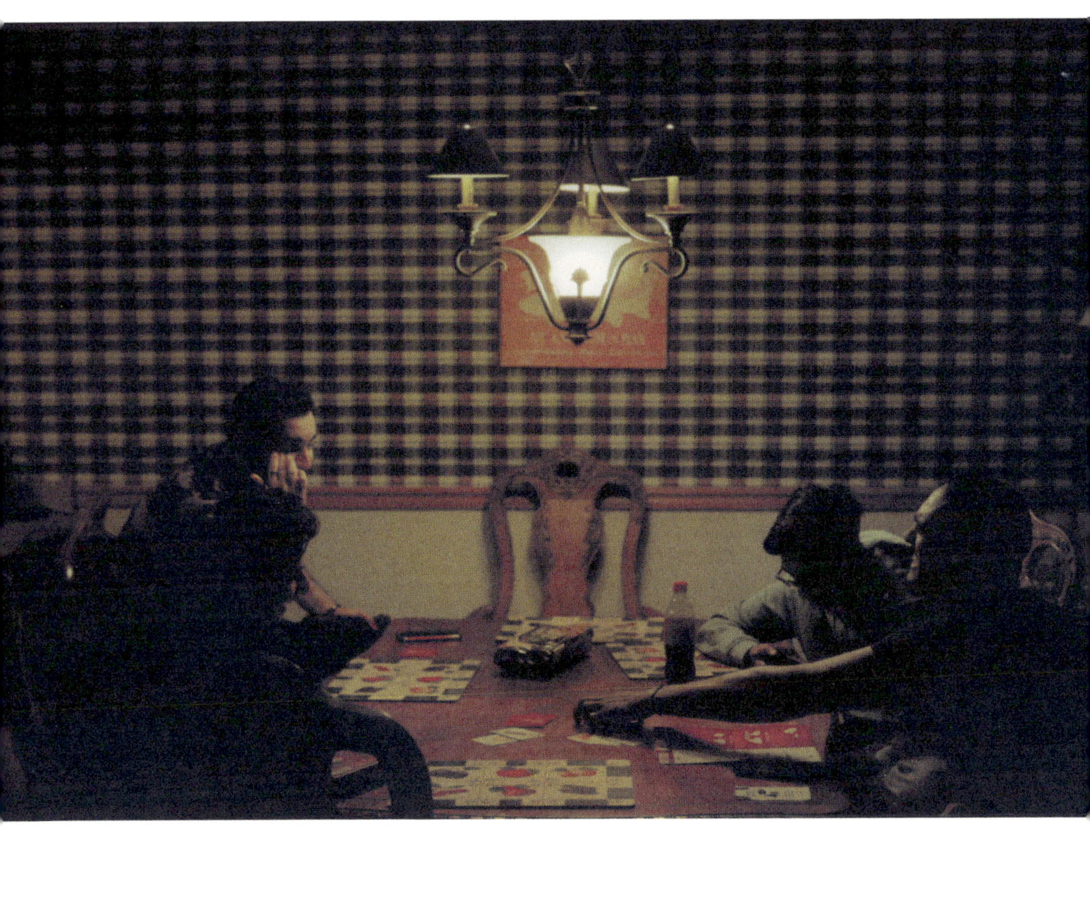

ALL OF US, TODAY

I am marveled at the way
the three of us stand in the kitchen,
speaking as if days before marriage and
children and divorce and leavings
had not existed. We become those kids,
who are gone but not gone, in the backyard
of the white shingled home before
we learned this nation's tongue.
I still live there. We were siblings
and children and nothing
more. Nothing more.

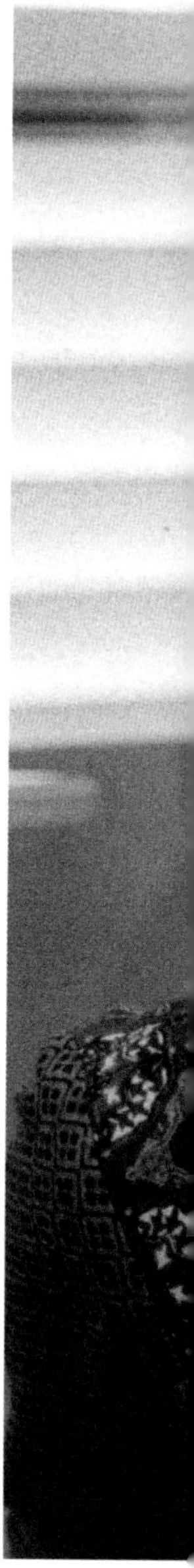

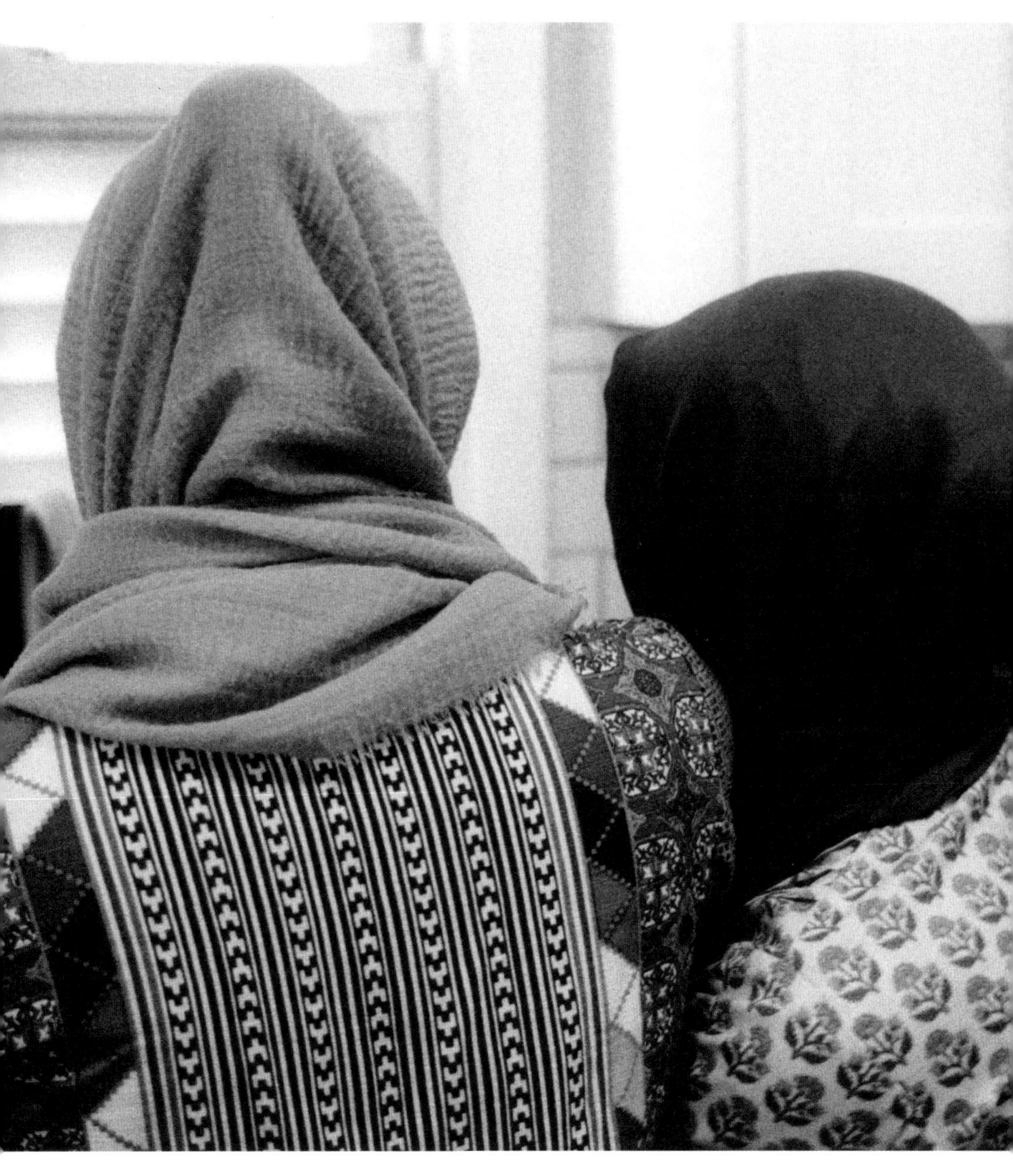

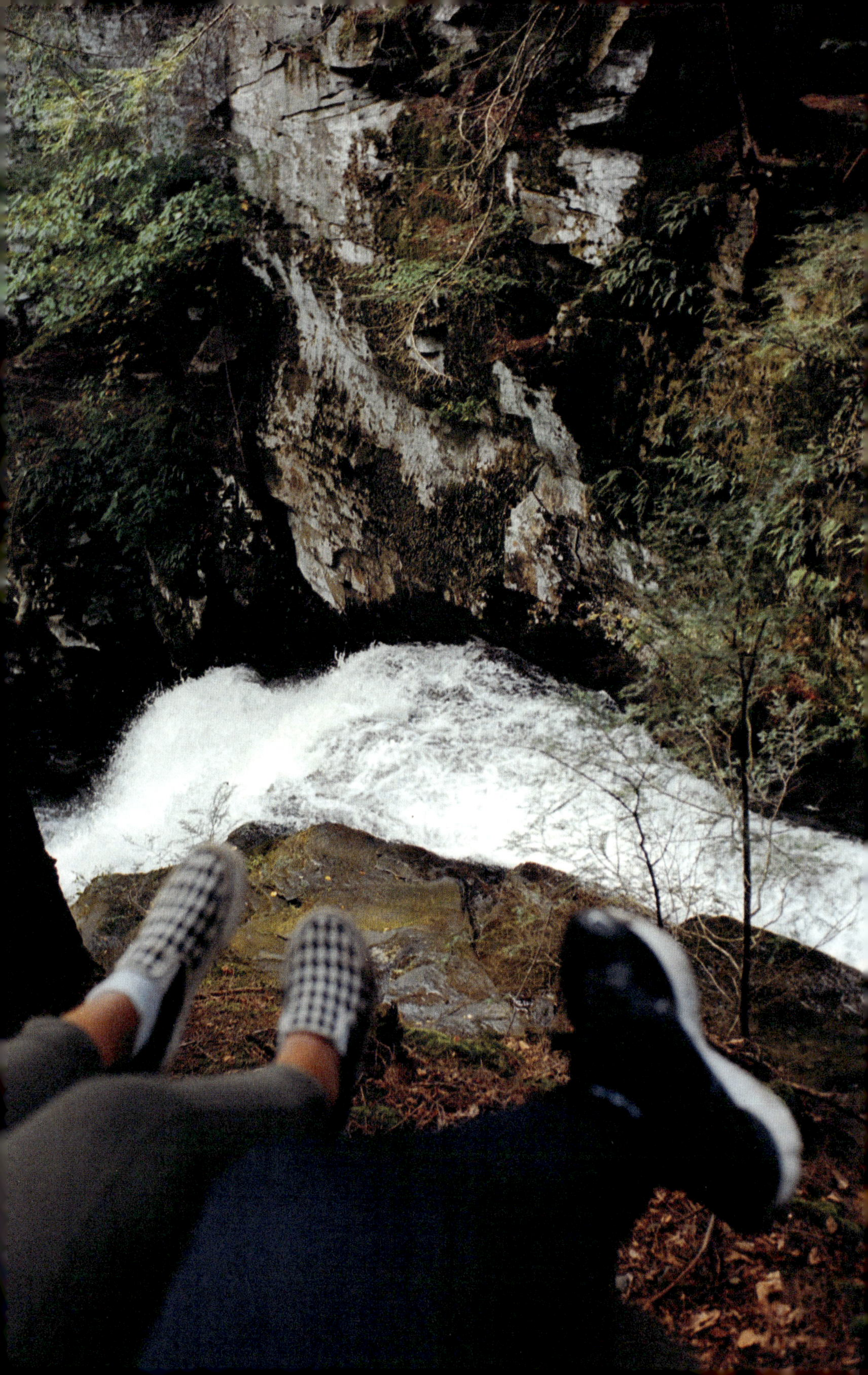

ON A HIKE

Our shoes are covered in mud
you hold me tight
the sun gazes at us through clouds

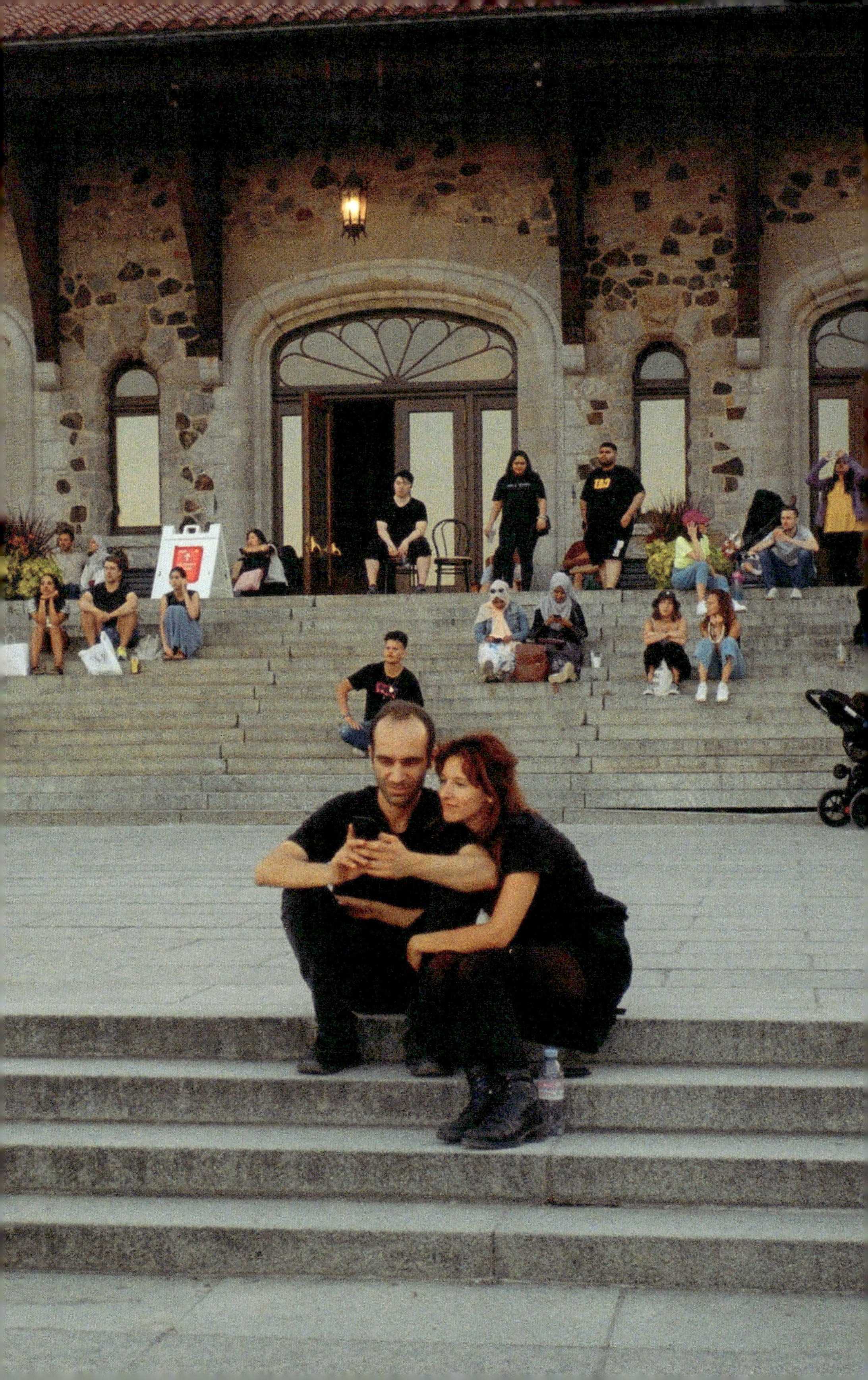

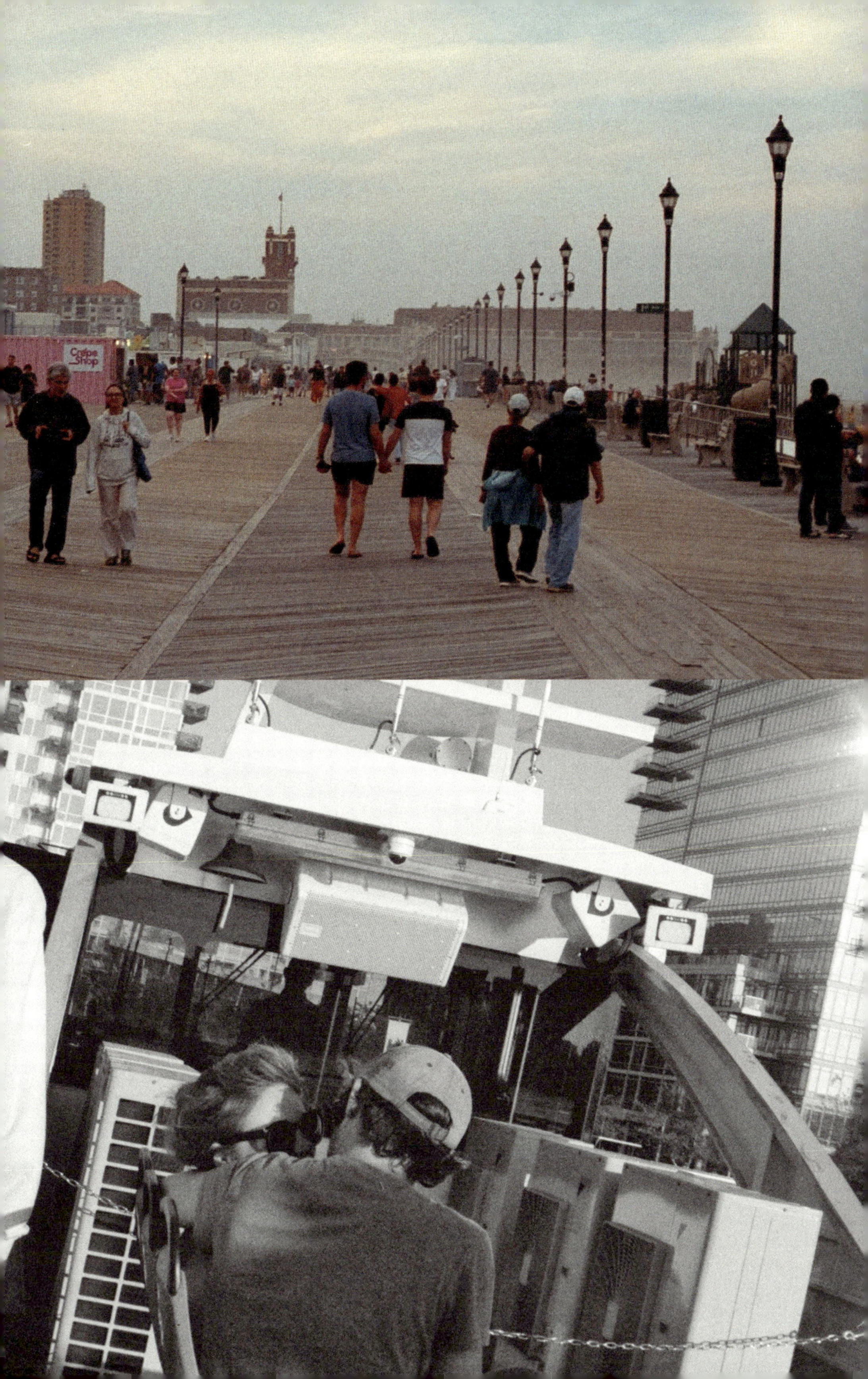
Crepe Shop

IN THE PHOTO BOOTH

I never thought
this would last

as long as it has. We sit
in a photo booth

on a heat-warning day
in June. Love does not evaporate

like the sweat on our skin. A countdown
flashes from three till the first picture

snaps as our clothes
stick heavy, the wetness cooling our skin

after the initial discomforting bends
of our bodies. Your fingers grace

my neck, the side of my head
on your wet cheek. A decade

gone. I did not know
I would be here. Next,

picture, you kiss me. I close
my eyes. Next

picture, I know
there are decades

to go. You stick your fingers
out, I make a heart with my thumb

and index finger. With the curtain
sliding open, we slowly begin

to develop,
my palms await arrival.

RELIVE WITH ME

In these moments when we
do not exist alongside one another, I hope
you decide to relive a time
when I rested within
your fondest memories.

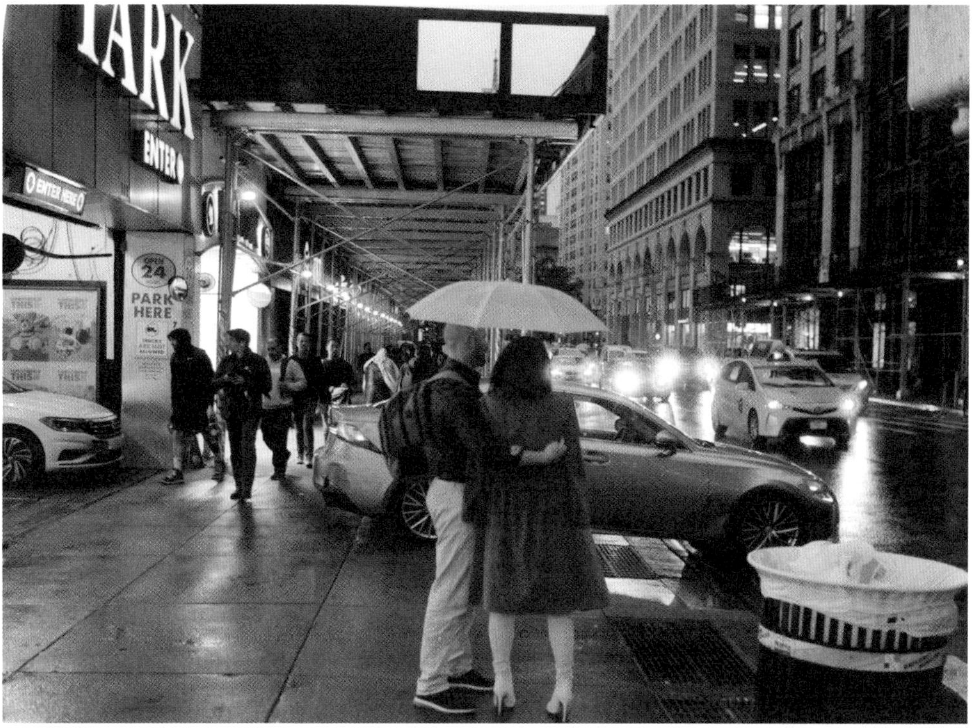

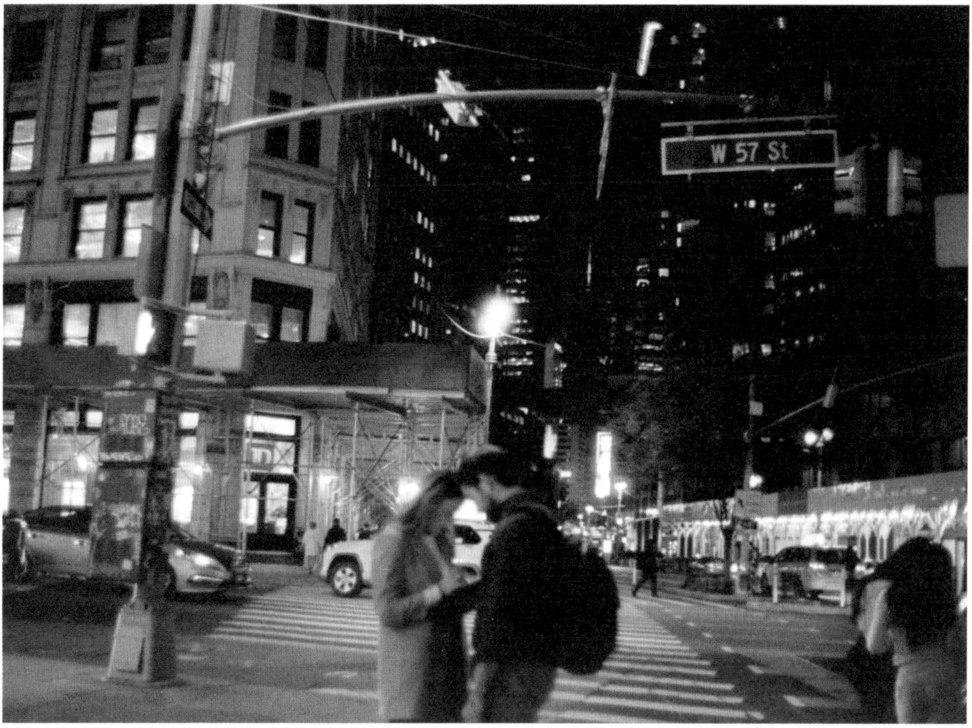

THOUGHTS BEFORE SUNRISE

All physical sensation
is incomparable to your touch. I find
it wearing to discover deeper
belonging elsewhere.

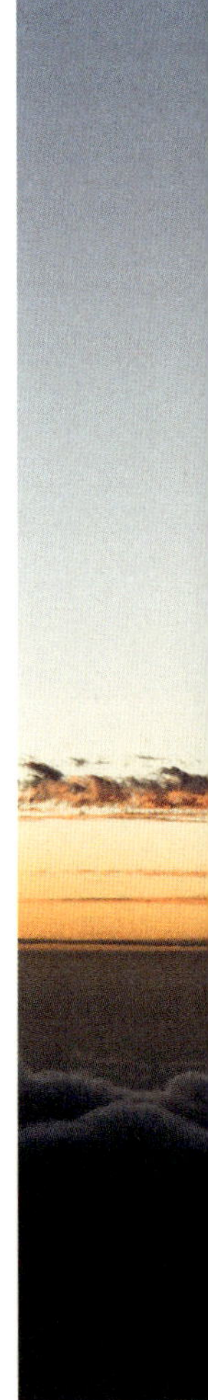

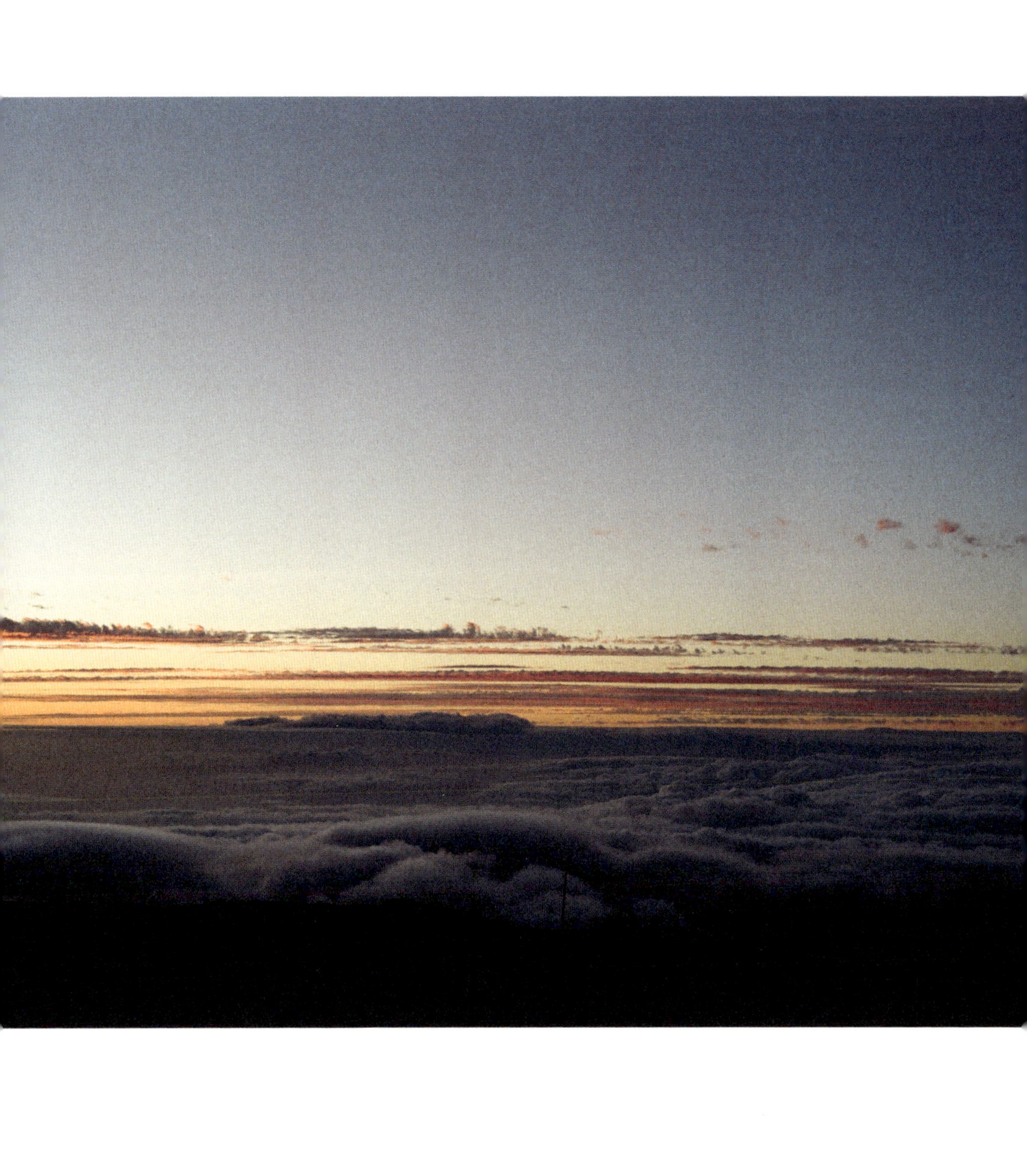

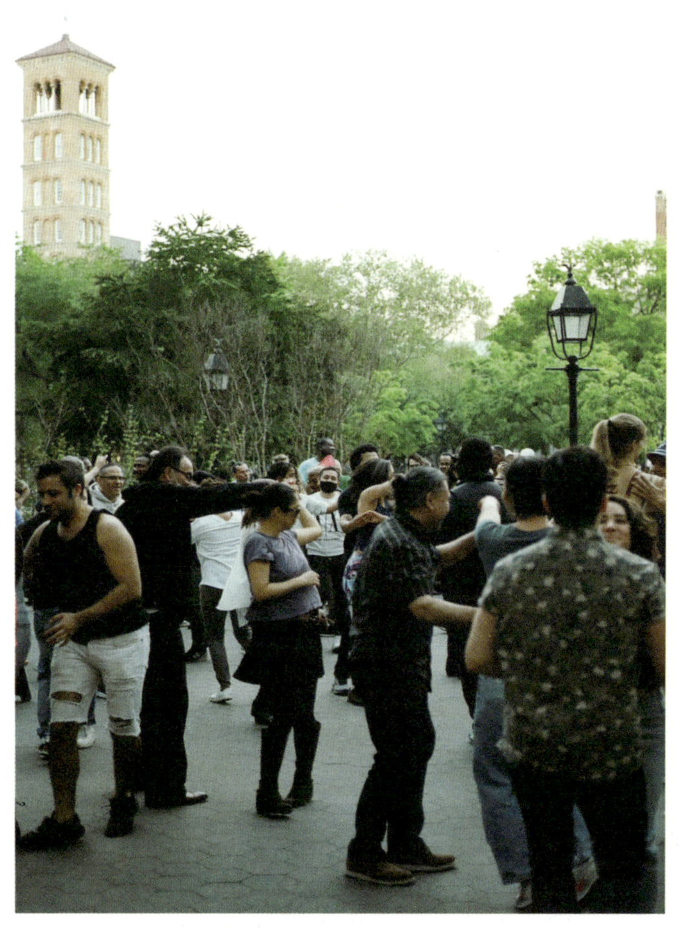

MOSAIC

In another lifetime, I hope to find more meaning in every movement. How a breath is not only a shared breath, but pieces of one another entering into our bodies. Collective mosaics of years lined up against our nerves made from encounters we've been graced with. How a bird is not a bird, but the embodied hope of one day being able to fly as far as we may need to, for ourselves. The ocean's vastness, how we cannot make out all the tears that've been shed into its body. Remnants of art drowning beneath the surface, becoming a shimmer the stars see themselves in. How in another lifetime, I hope I find you in the expansive crowd and we recognize the art we've shared with one another, a showcase for just us.

THE SOFT HUM

It is possible, I suppose, to look off into
the horizon with ache. A pang of discomfort
and a foreign emotion that even you may
not know how to pronounce its letterings.

I look down and your index finger traces
the words—each shape unwinding from the last.

Every letter on my tongue,
my fingers touch its damp softness.

It is also possible, I suppose, to finally
be able to hear the soft hum

that resides between our trees.

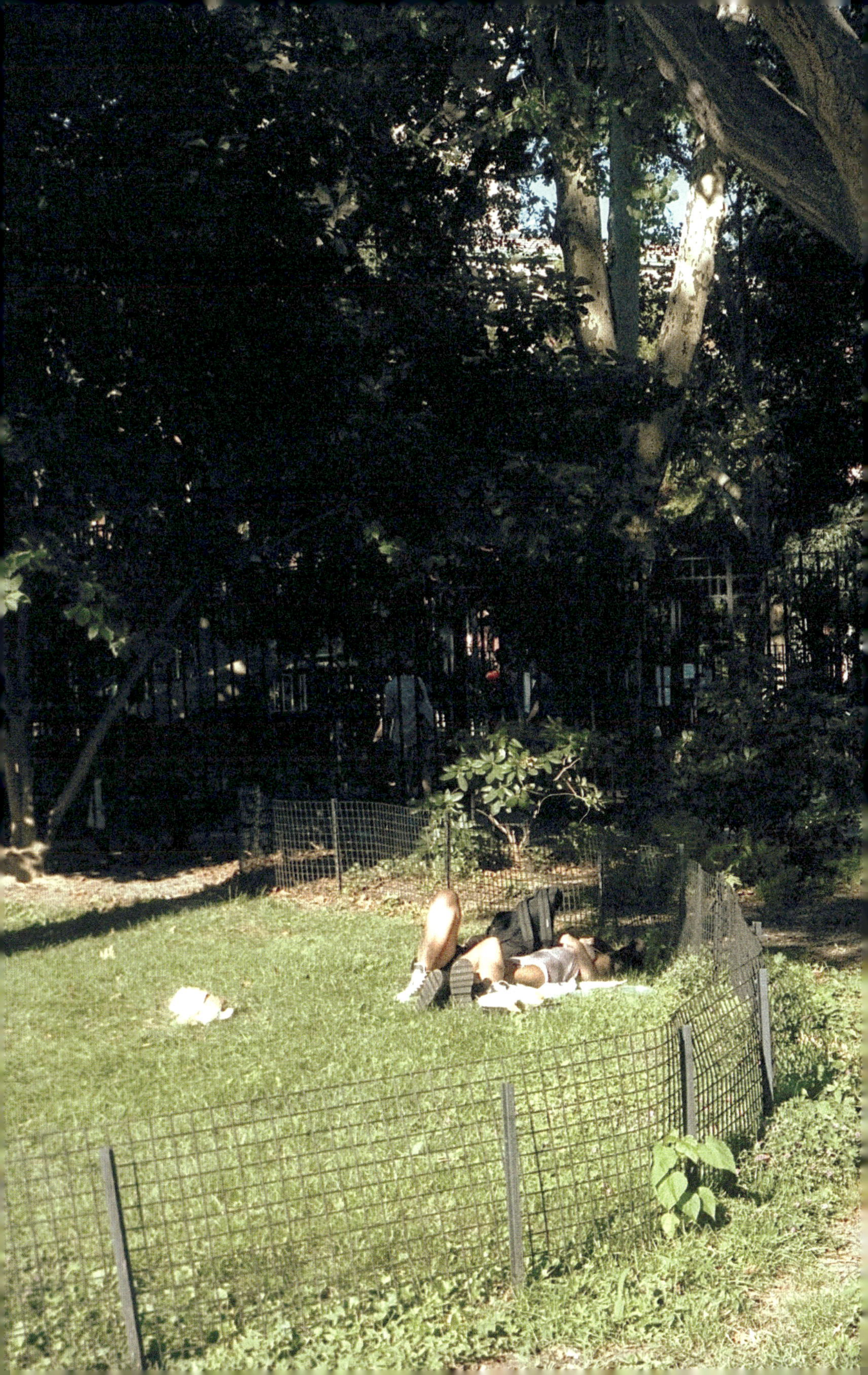

Love and resistance have always gone hand in hand. Without one, the other would cease to exist.

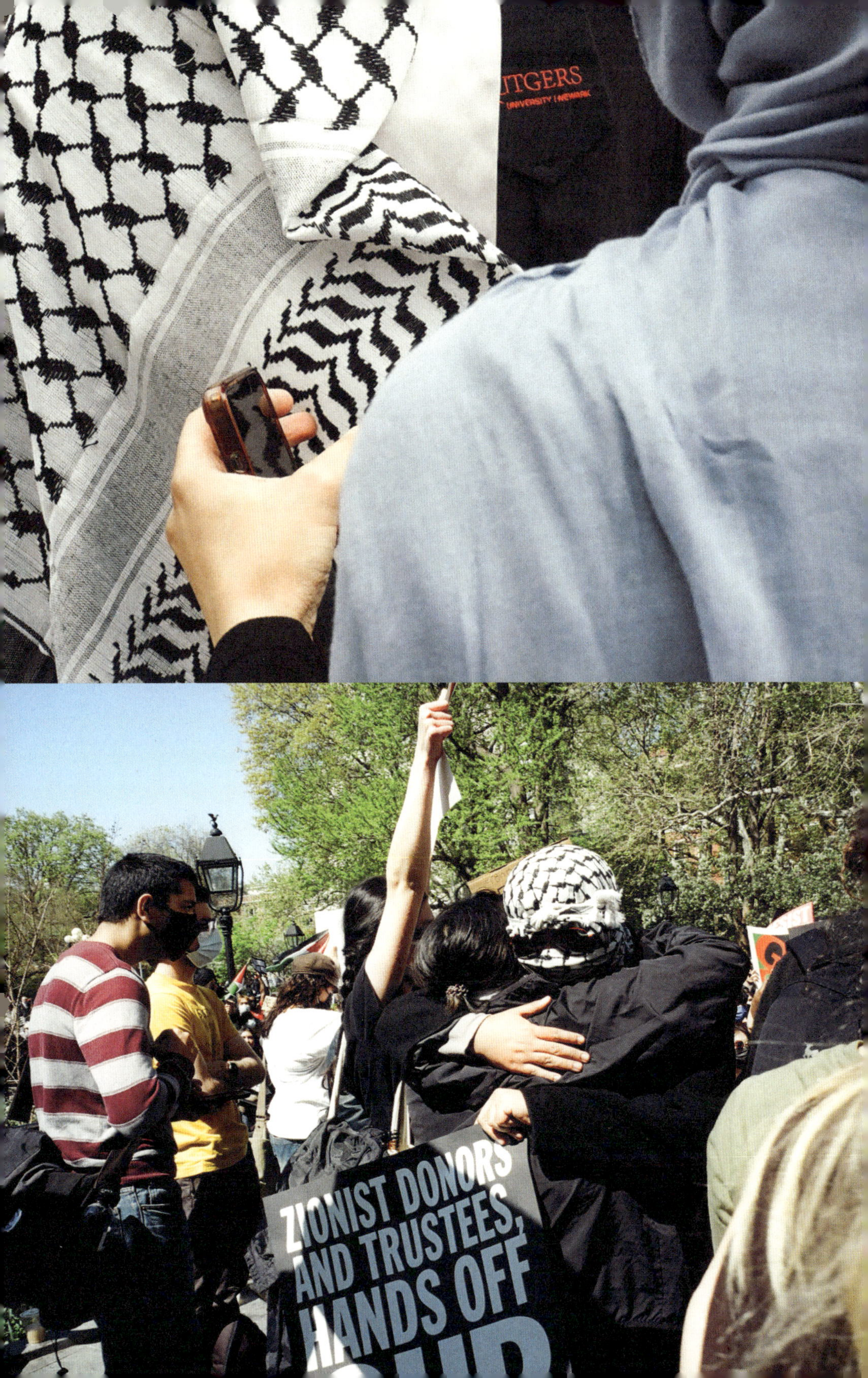
ITGERS
ZIONIST DONORS
AND TRUSTEES,
HANDS OFF

NOOR AND NOOR

It's taken years for me
to adjust to the light you bring
into my life. But I can say for certain
that I am growing to accept it.

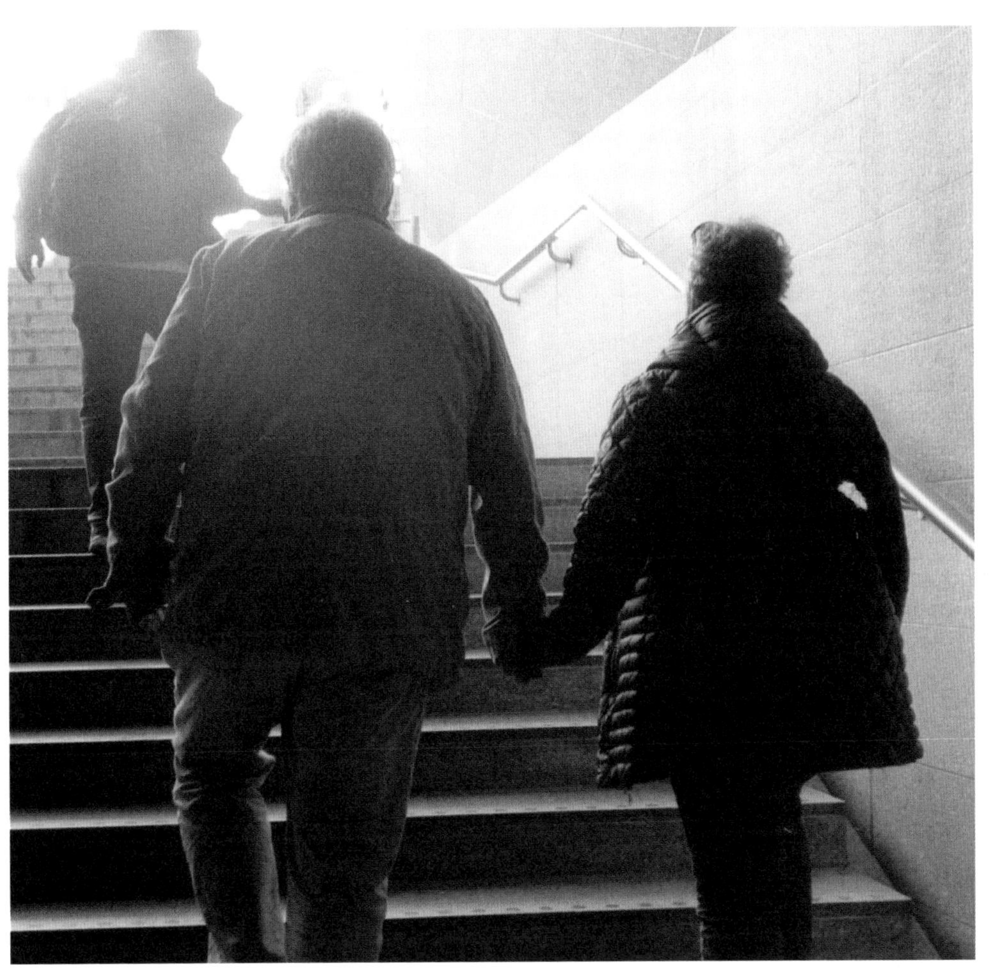

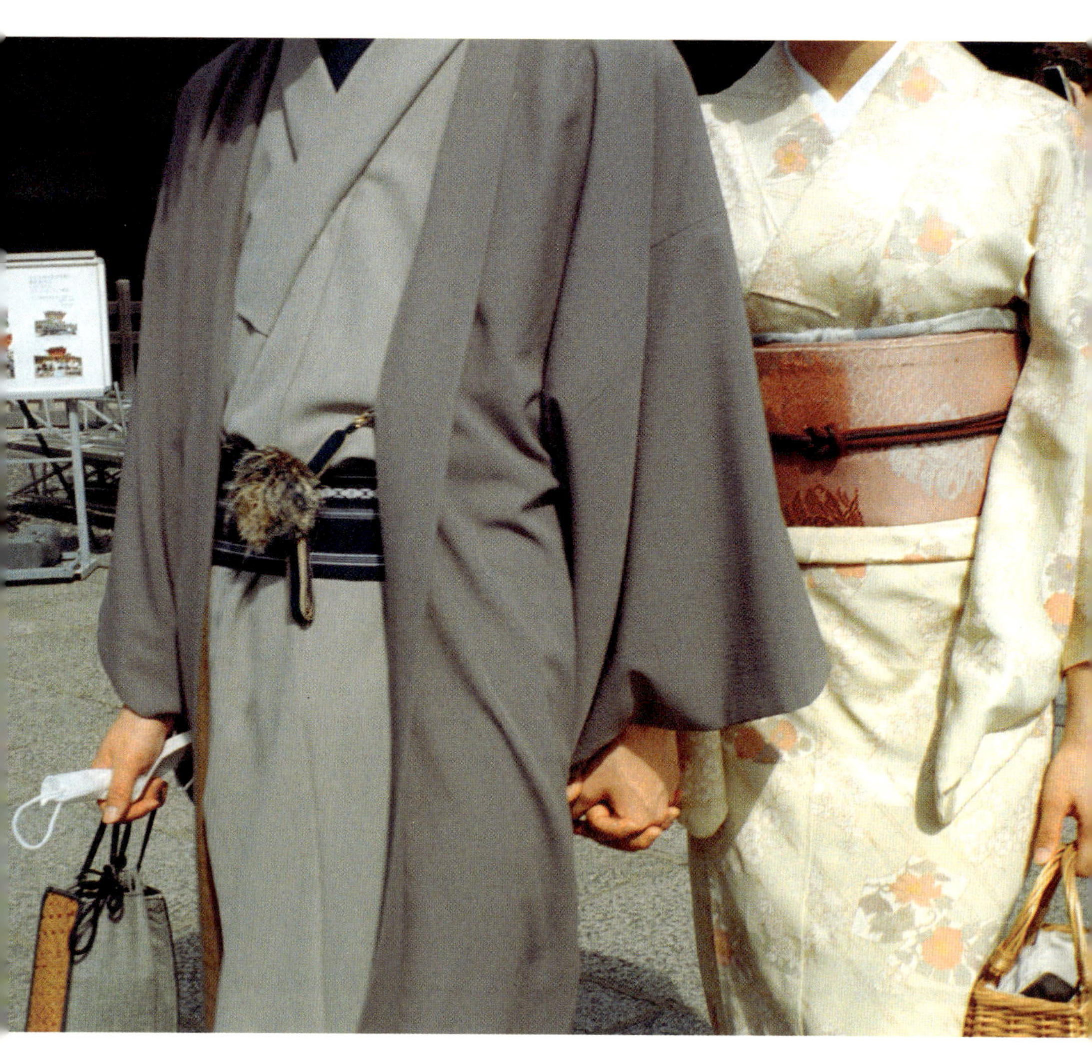

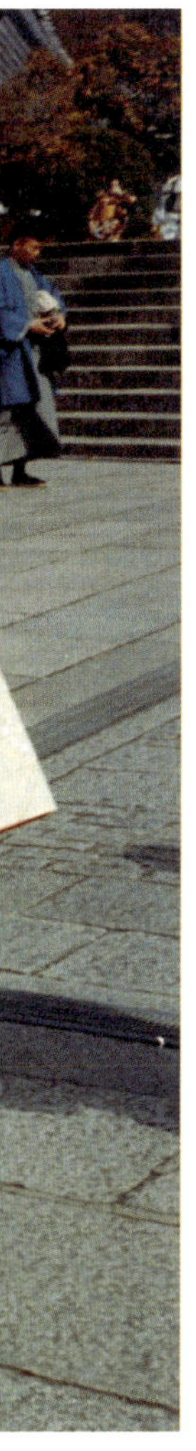

WITHOUT BREAKING

In all our years, we have
stood by each other. Like statues
carved from the same slab,
we know full existence without one another
cannot exist.

EXISTENCE IS TIRING

For the many days
I struggle to exist,
I know I can lean on you
to carry me.

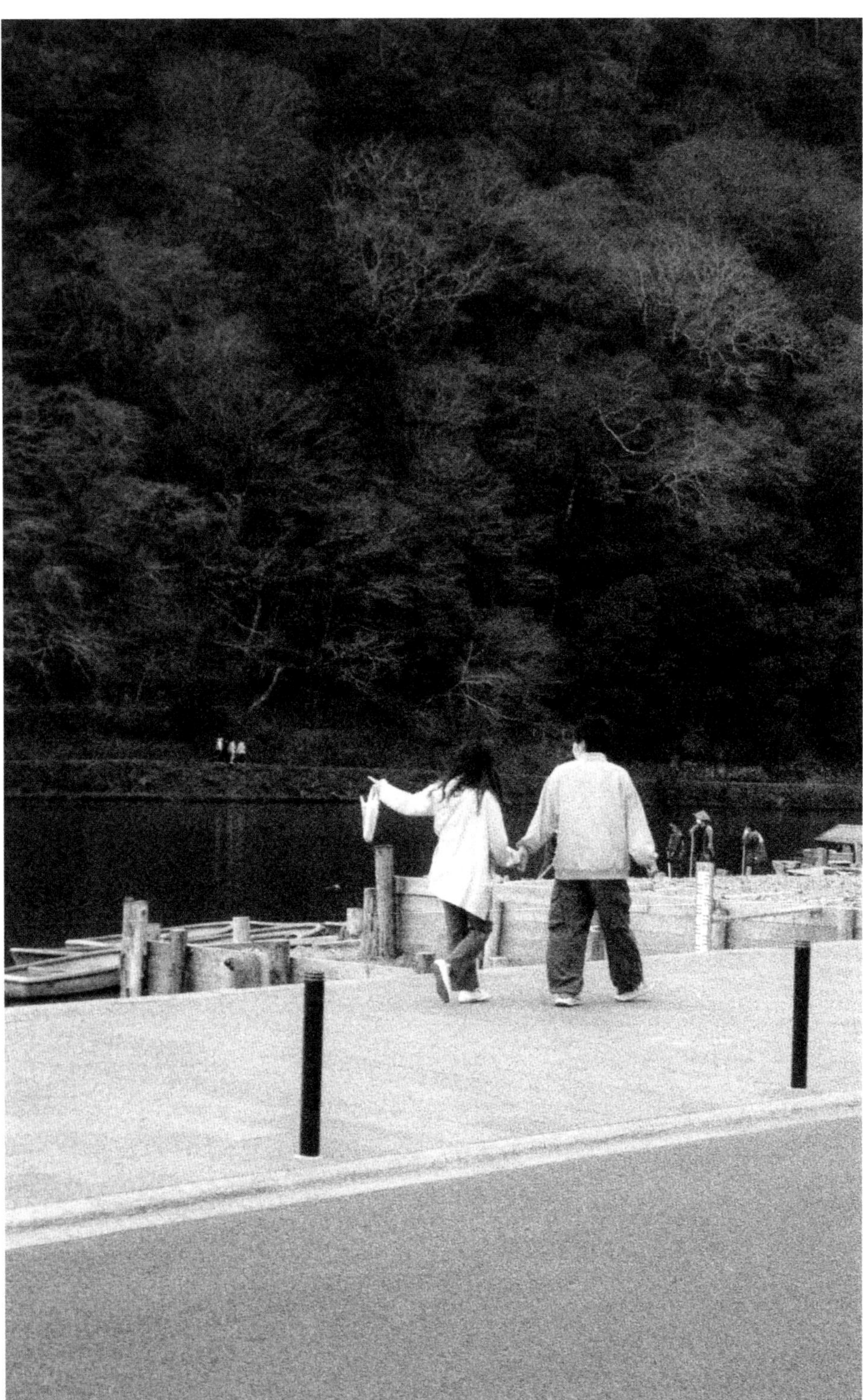

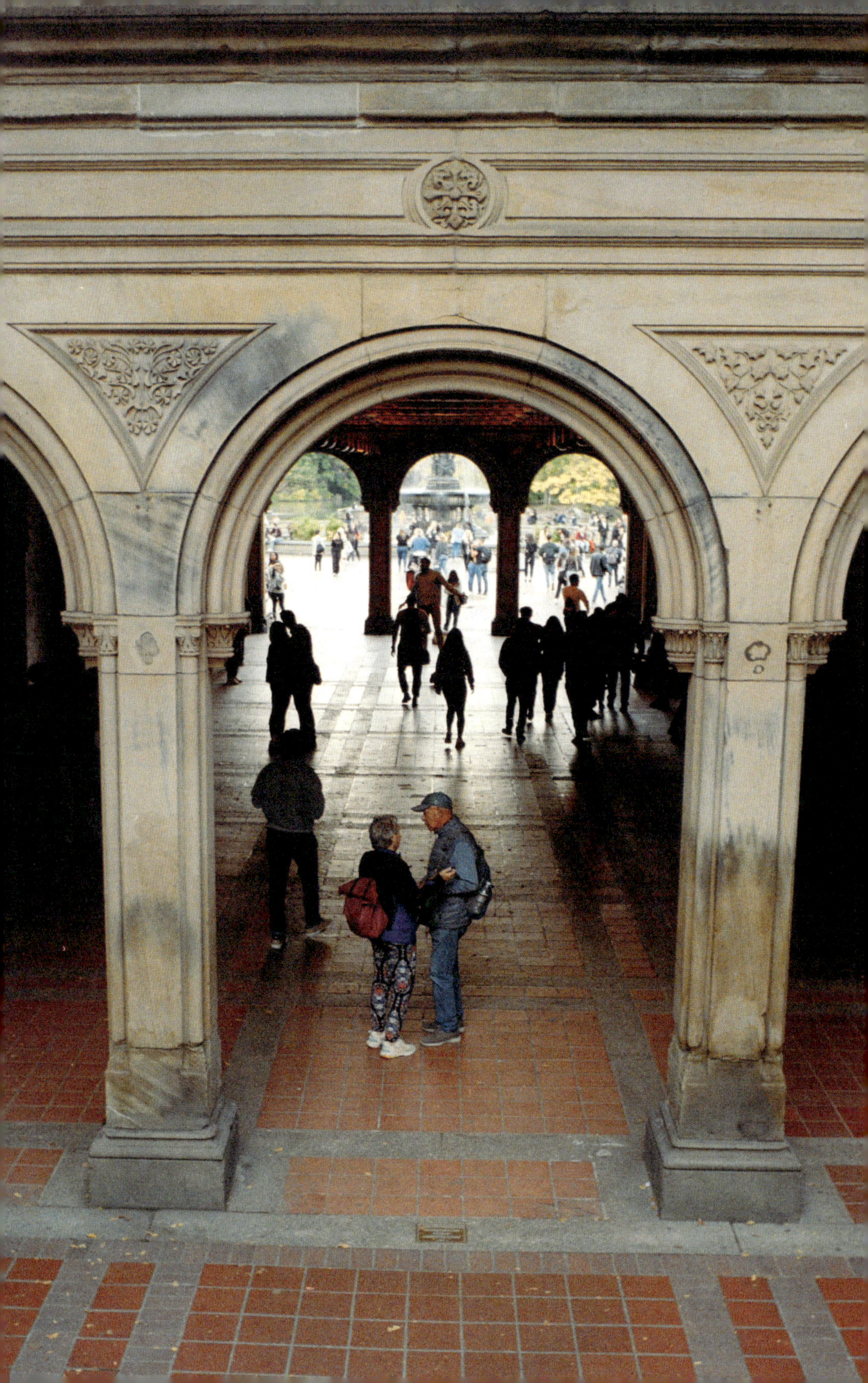

THE REASON

I desperately capture
endearment that exists around me,
so when I look back, I understand
I was surrounded by warmth.

CARRYING THIS LOVE

All these negatives become
unwritten letters I sign to myself.
Years later, when I peel open
these pictures, I will be reminded
of how dense this love is and how
we cannot carry all of it ourselves.

WITH NOTHING COMES EVERYTHING

I will never tire of
you walking through the door,
eyes wide and smile bountiful.
Even if I have nothing else,
this will be etched into my being.

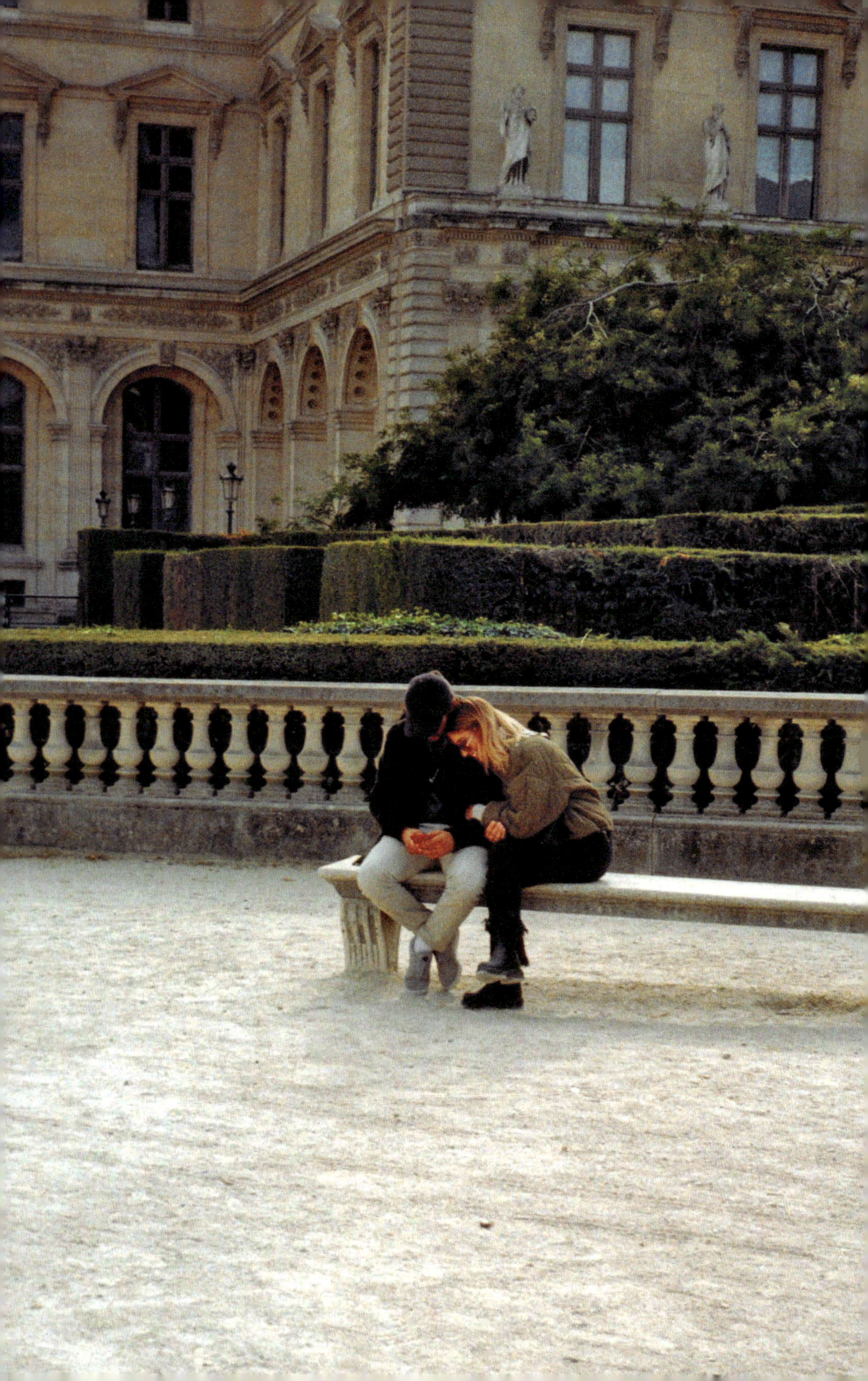

WHAT WILL NOT EXIST

You have grounded me—have I told you that? All my life, I have been moving, everyday moments disrupted with inconsistencies of those around me. To always plan for an ending even though I was just beginning. I got used to how loud life was. How there was nothing more than the noise and nothing past the next disruption. Until you held on to me. Telling me to stop thinking and planning and what life would look like after us, because that didn't, and wouldn't, exist.

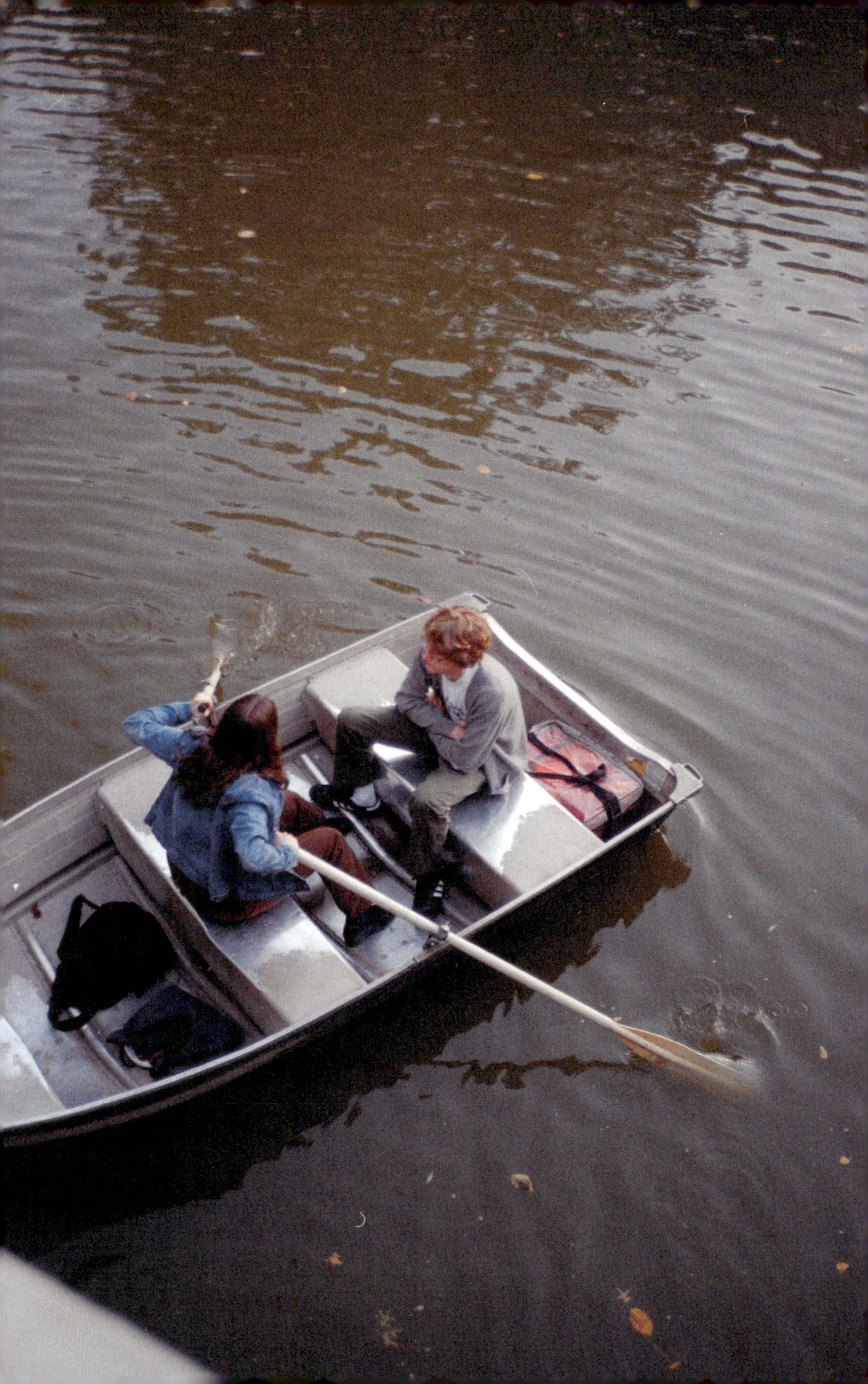

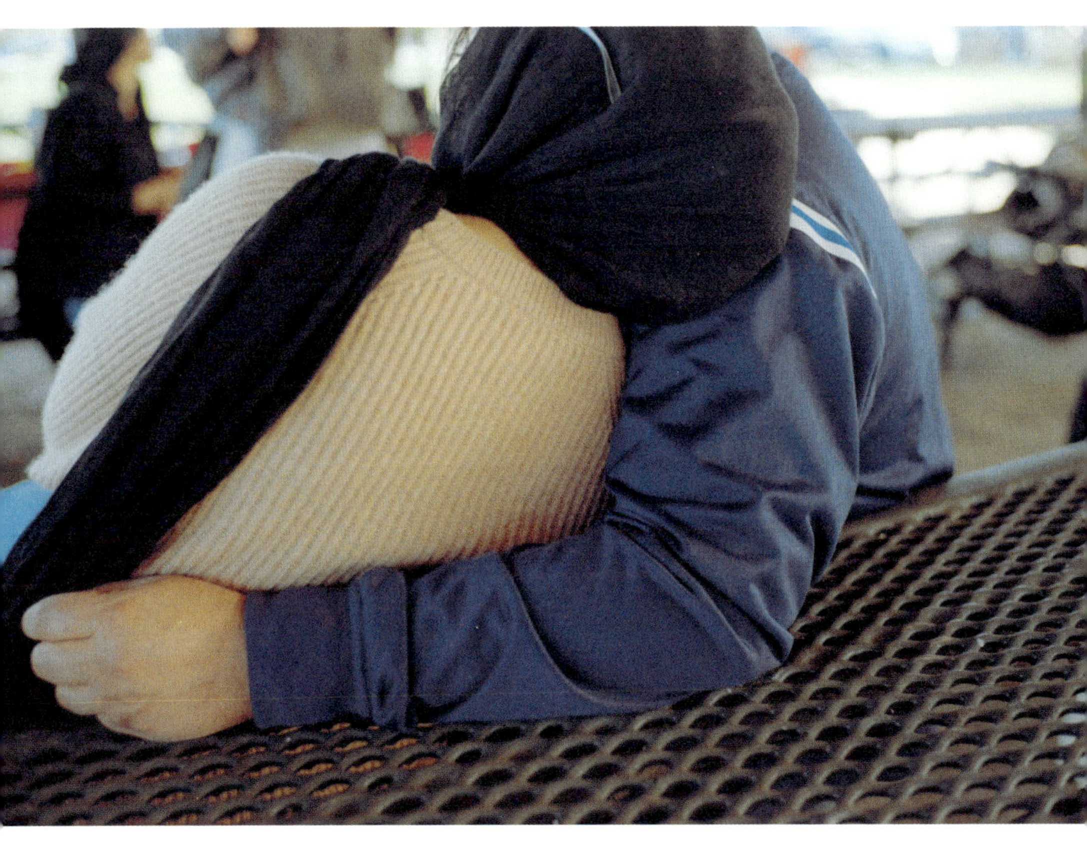

YOU KNOW ME MORE

When all is lost, I begin
to look toward you. You've not only guided
me, but know exactly of my needs
when I do not know them myself.

SMITHEREENS

Behind the shuttered blinds, resting in one another's arms, I'd like to think that our existence is minimal. That no one knows of us here—no one sees us. That outside our home, even if the whole world has fallen to smithereens, we would still have the sanctuary that we've built together.

CLOUD'S EYE VIEW

We lie in greenery that reaches between our ears and the cicadas sing toward one another. We stare at the clouds passing above and I imagine being one. To move places without a care or worry—to see you from time to time. In our current silence, I want you to know that my heart tends to stay empty most days. You fill it at this hour. The yearning to leave leaves. The desire to mold myself so I can't recall my own name evaporates only because you won't recognize me. You've filled me enough for the sun's purity to witness. Enough for the greenery that's swaying against our skin to attach onto our pores. Enough for me to see you, and only you, as the clouds pass.

And whenever I hear cicadas sing, I'm greeted by your remembrance.

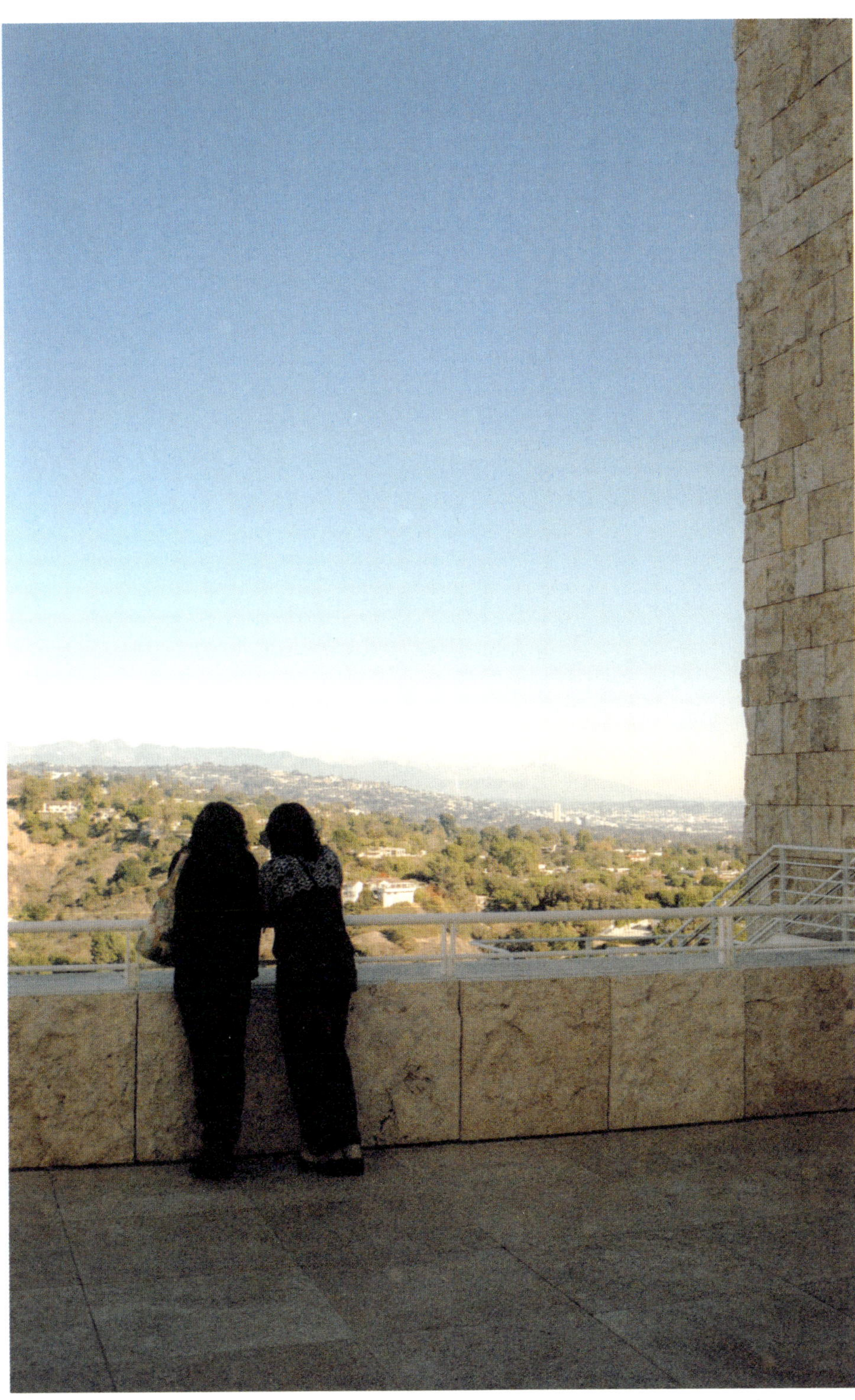

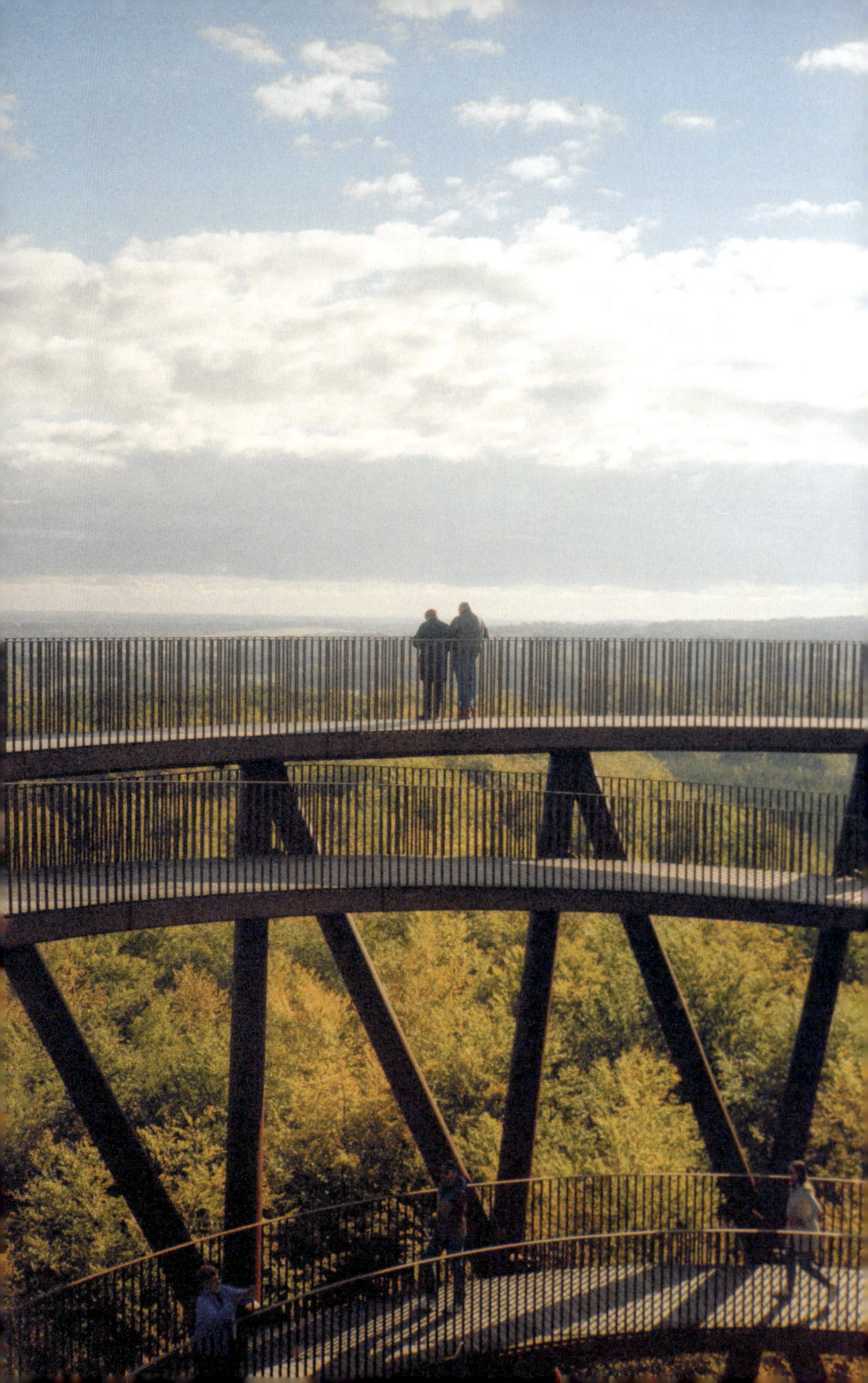

FROM YEARS AGO

Though I miss our once-new passion,
I have learned that tenderness
is ever-growing, shifting with
our bodies and the passing time.
With change, we must relearn
the many ways to nurture our bond.

PUSHING THROUGH THE CRACKS

In my younger years, I believed
there to be a concrete ceiling over
me. That love would always have
a limit it would refuse to push past.

Yet, it's seeped its way in-between
the cracks—filling the skies above
with shades I'm slowly learning
the names of.

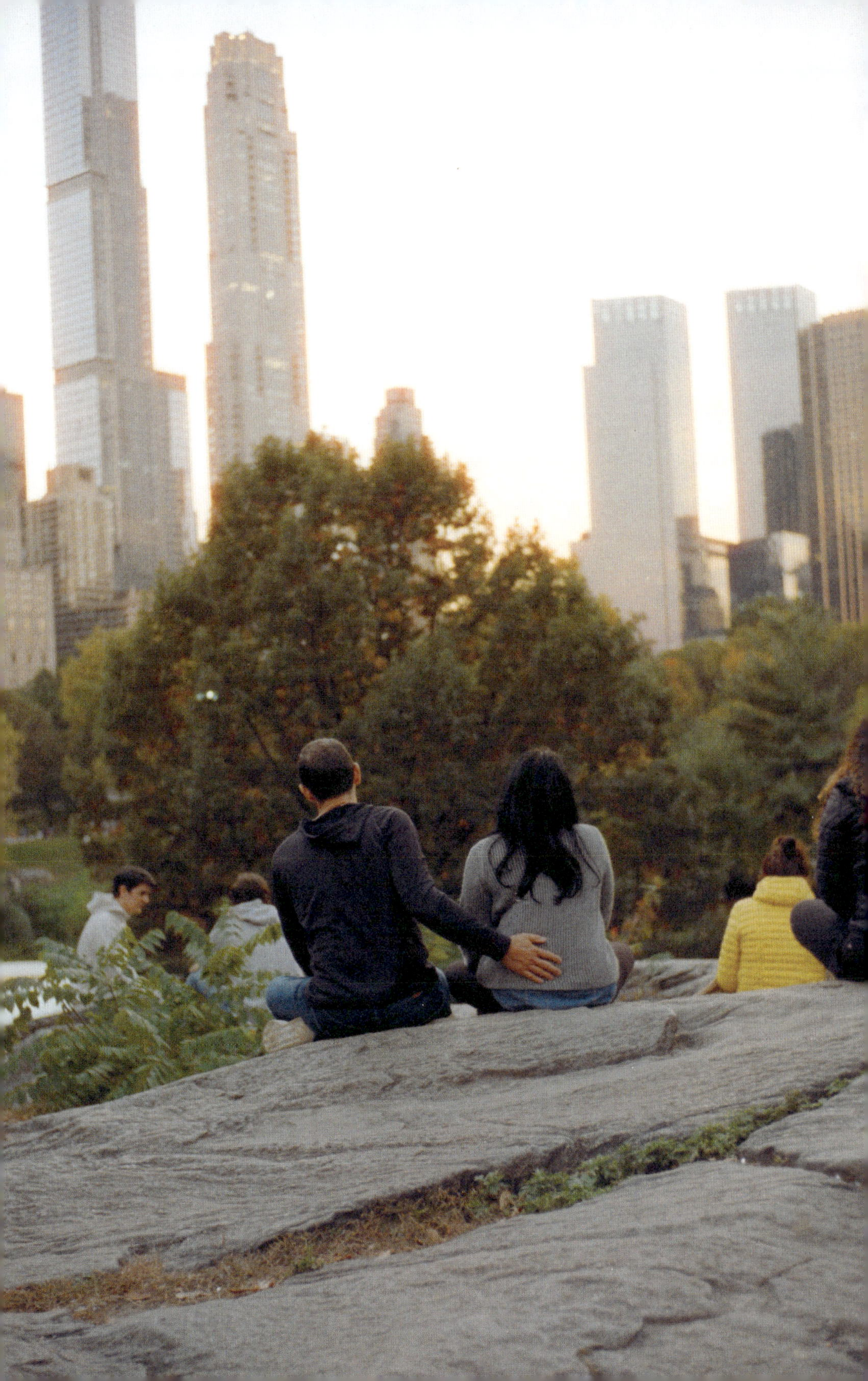

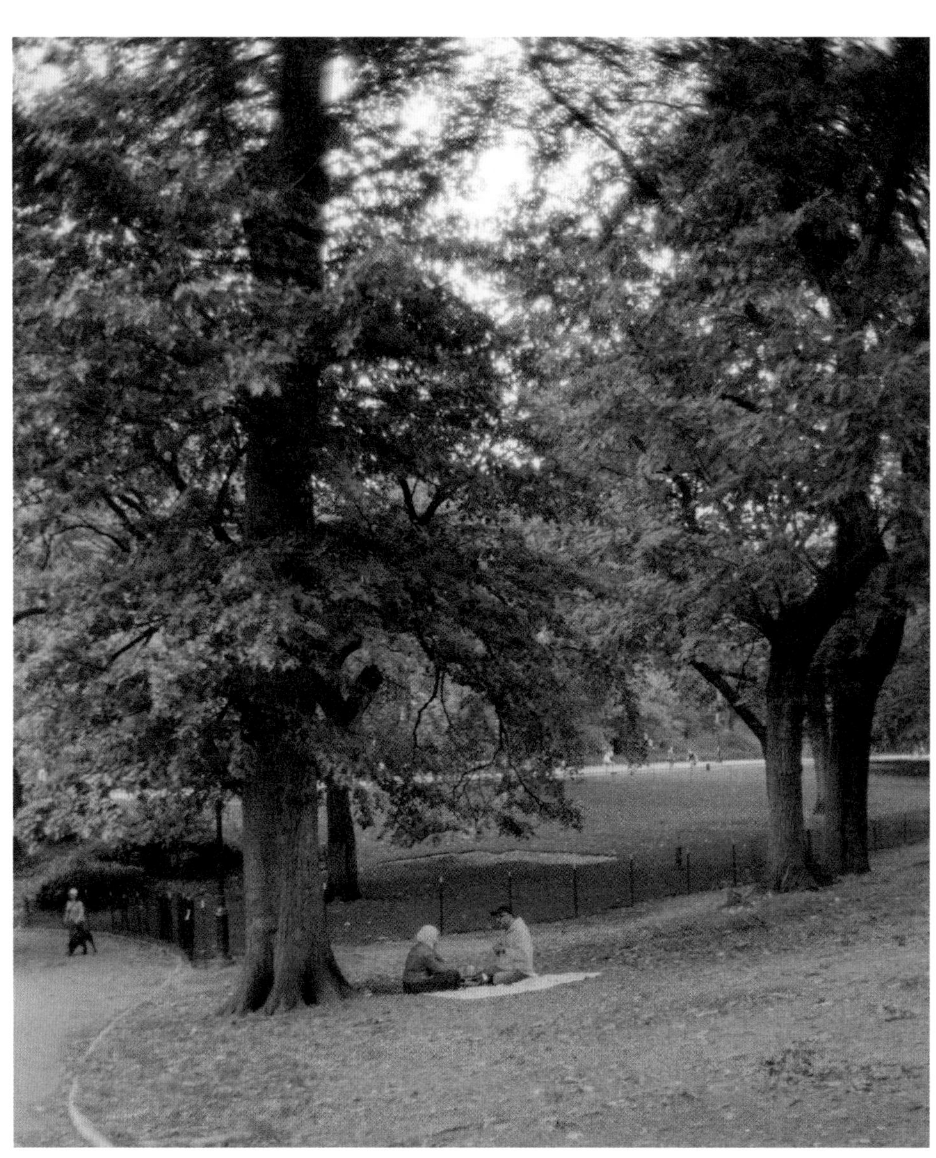

HOLD MY HEART CLOSE

There are things you can't
reach—even with your hands in their
chest. How they hold half

of your heart and nothing
more. Nothing more. A flower stem split
open between your fingers, and

dryness meeting them. You notice
then how much time you've given to
another that was never going

to give what they owe. Yet,
the flower sprouts, and you give
and give   and give.

hold me tightly,
so I know this is real.
so I know I am real.

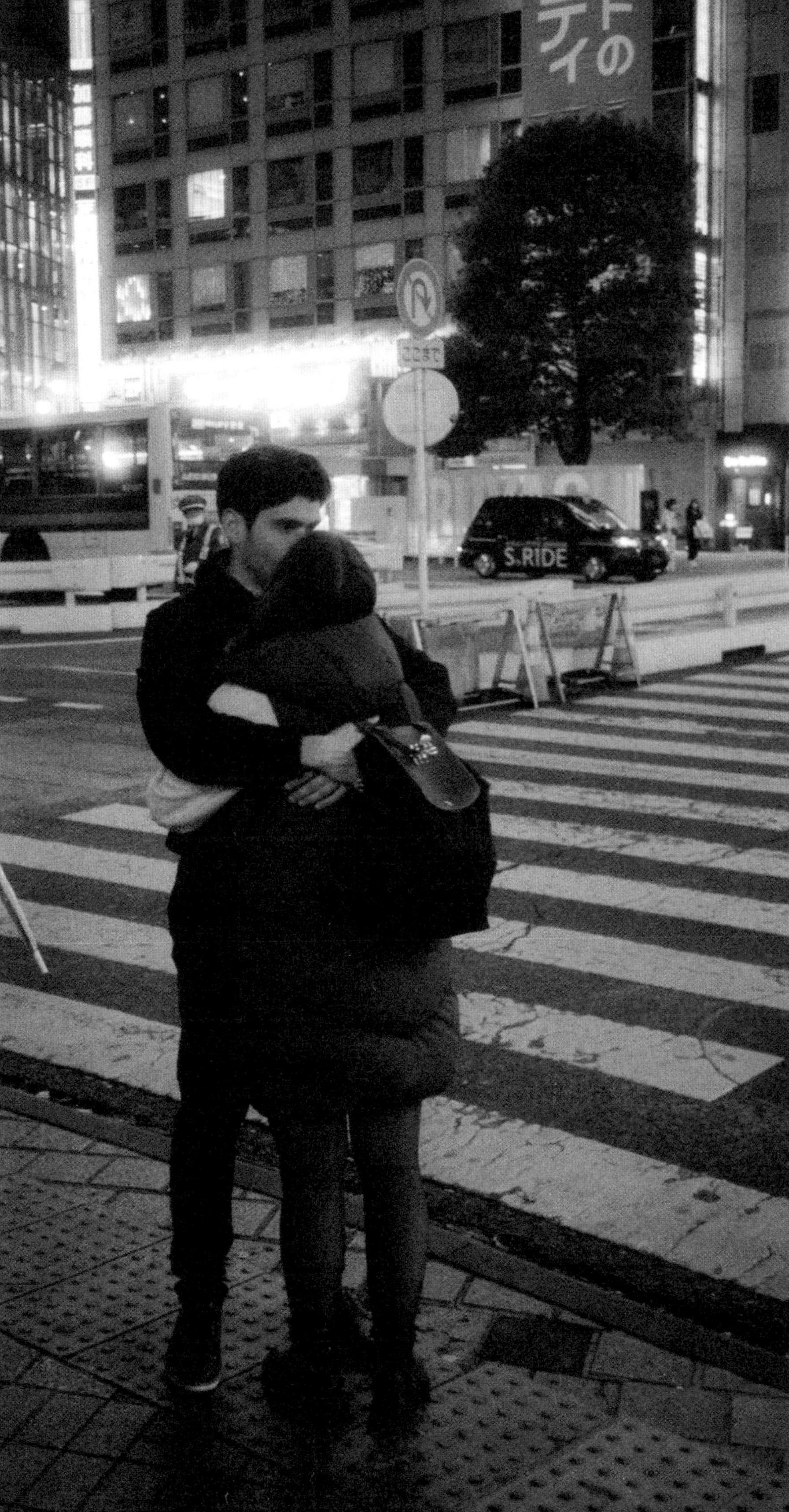
S.RIDE

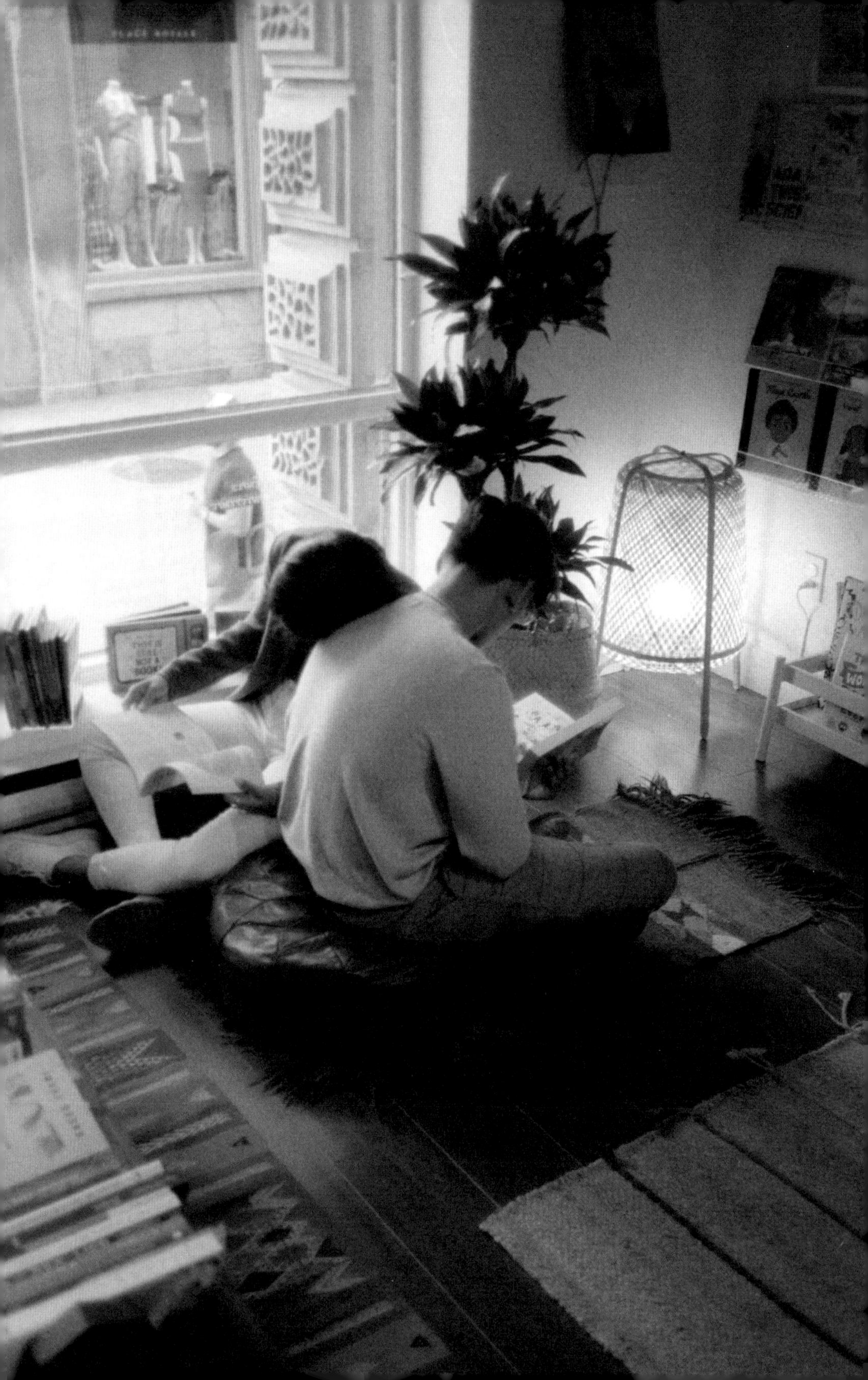

SEPTEMBER READINGS

Smell of fresh paper and unwrapped
books as two people sit on colored pillows,
her head resting on his shoulder
as she reads and his angled

down. It's September and you hold
my hand a bit tighter, squeezing it
whenever my name leaves your mouth.
With retreating heat, the forthcoming

cold. You ask me if I remember
our history and I tell you
it smells of old paper and drying ink,
still in the process of being written.

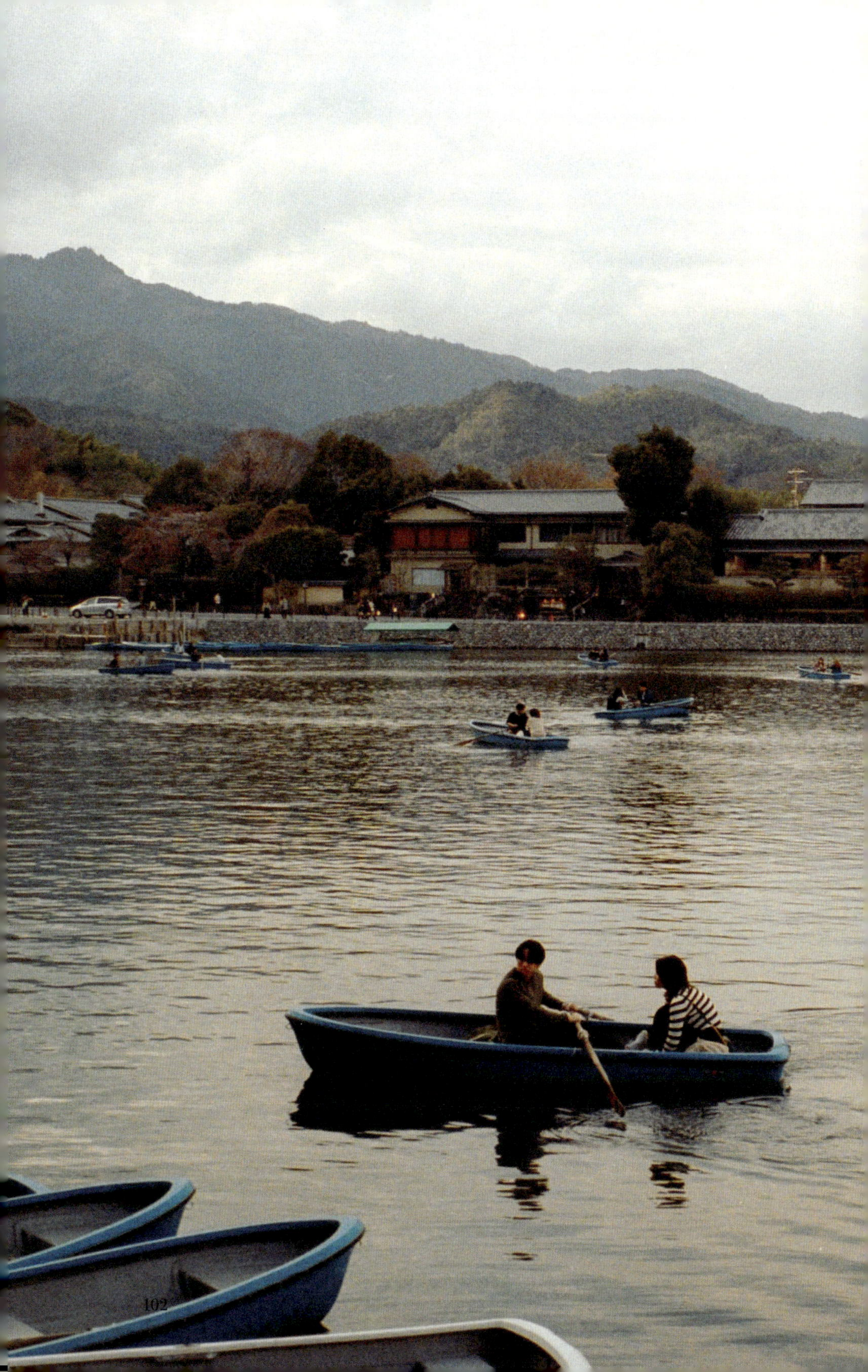

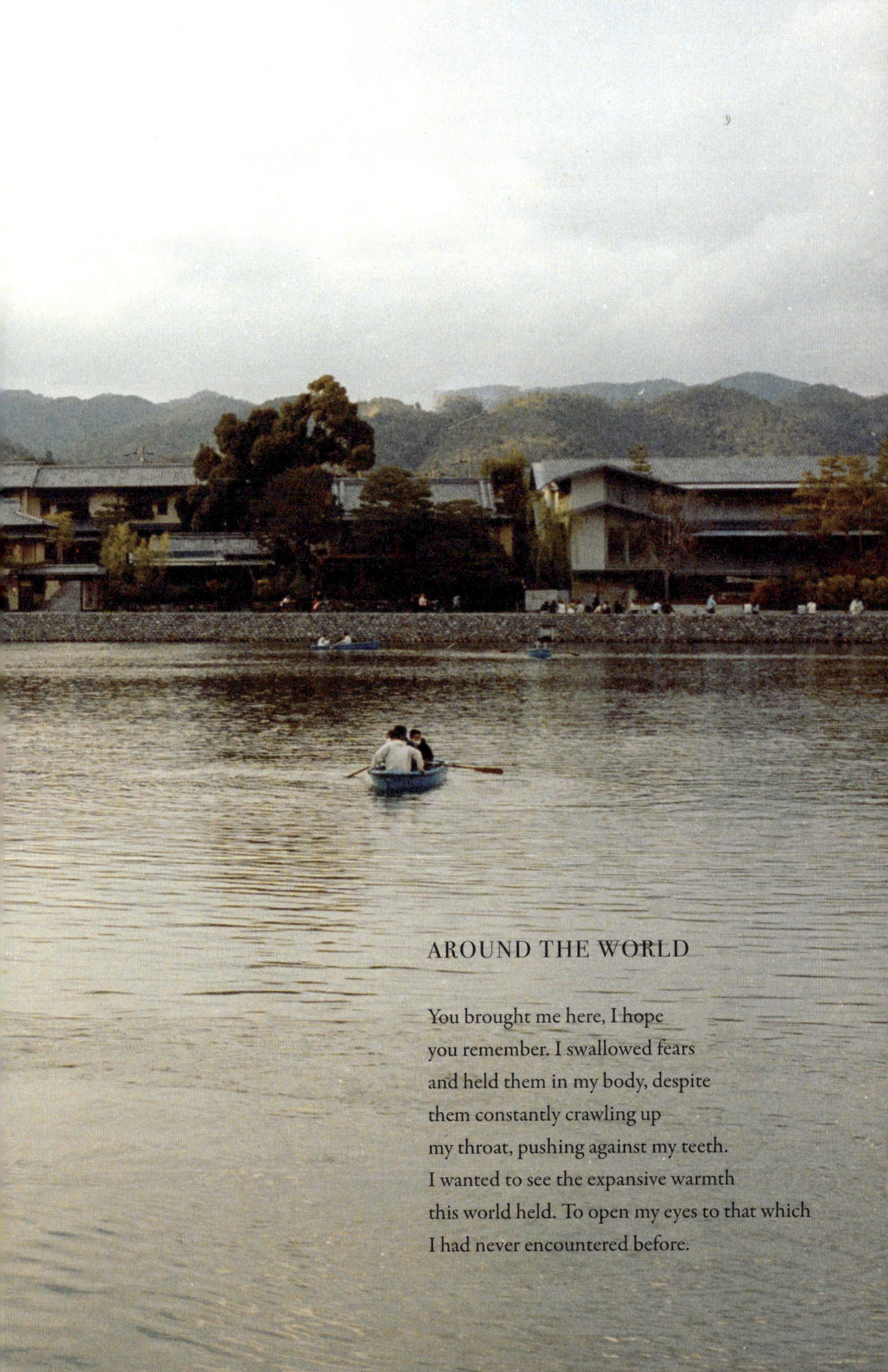

AROUND THE WORLD

You brought me here, I hope
you remember. I swallowed fears
and held them in my body, despite
them constantly crawling up
my throat, pushing against my teeth.
I wanted to see the expansive warmth
this world held. To open my eyes to that which
I had never encountered before.

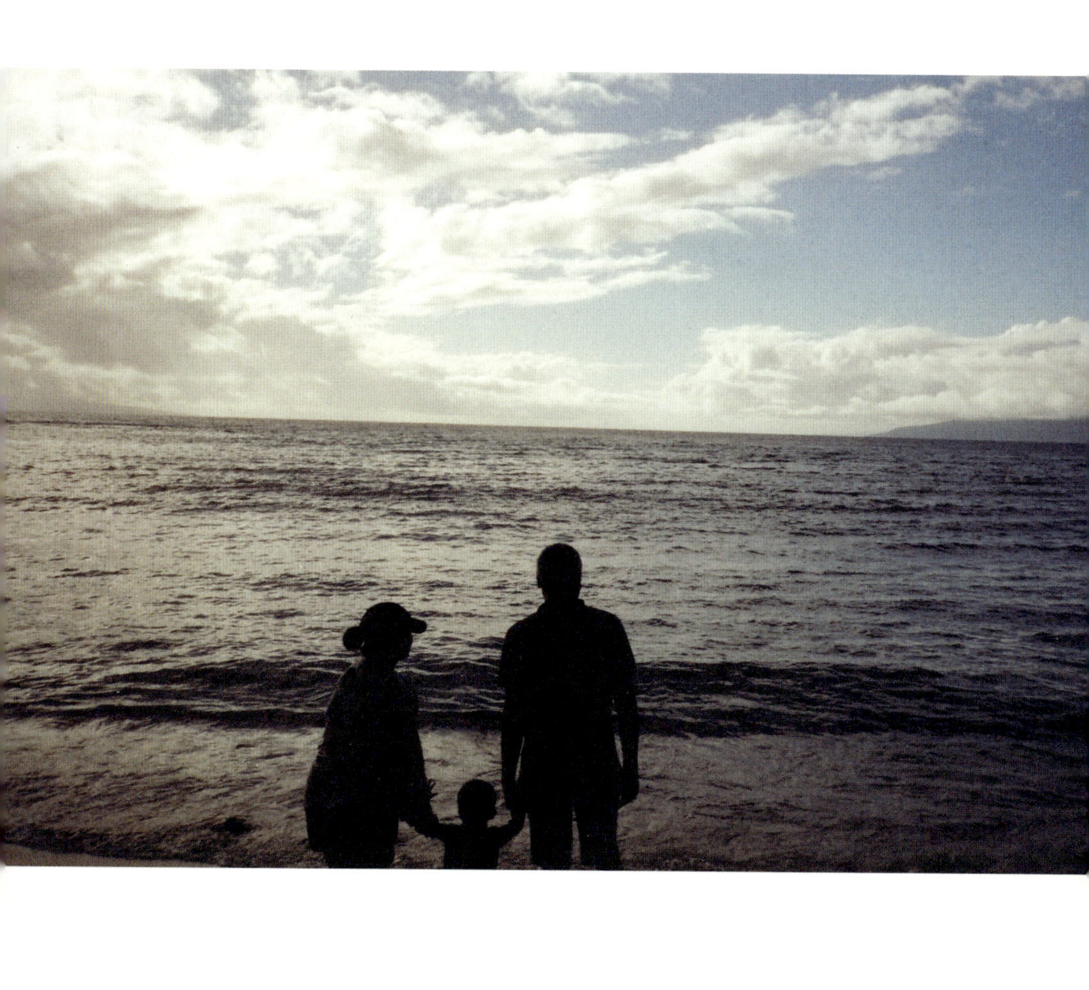

AFTERWARD, WE HOPE MORE

I'd like to see you again
by the ocean. Our feet buried in the sand,
overlooking existence.

How this life felt eternal,
even though both of us have
seen its truth. We pick up shells
that lodge themselves

in our soles. We ask for their journey. Wonder how much
more life is to be lived. Muse on how long
we can call heaven

upon one another. We hope and hope
                                        until our eyes shut.

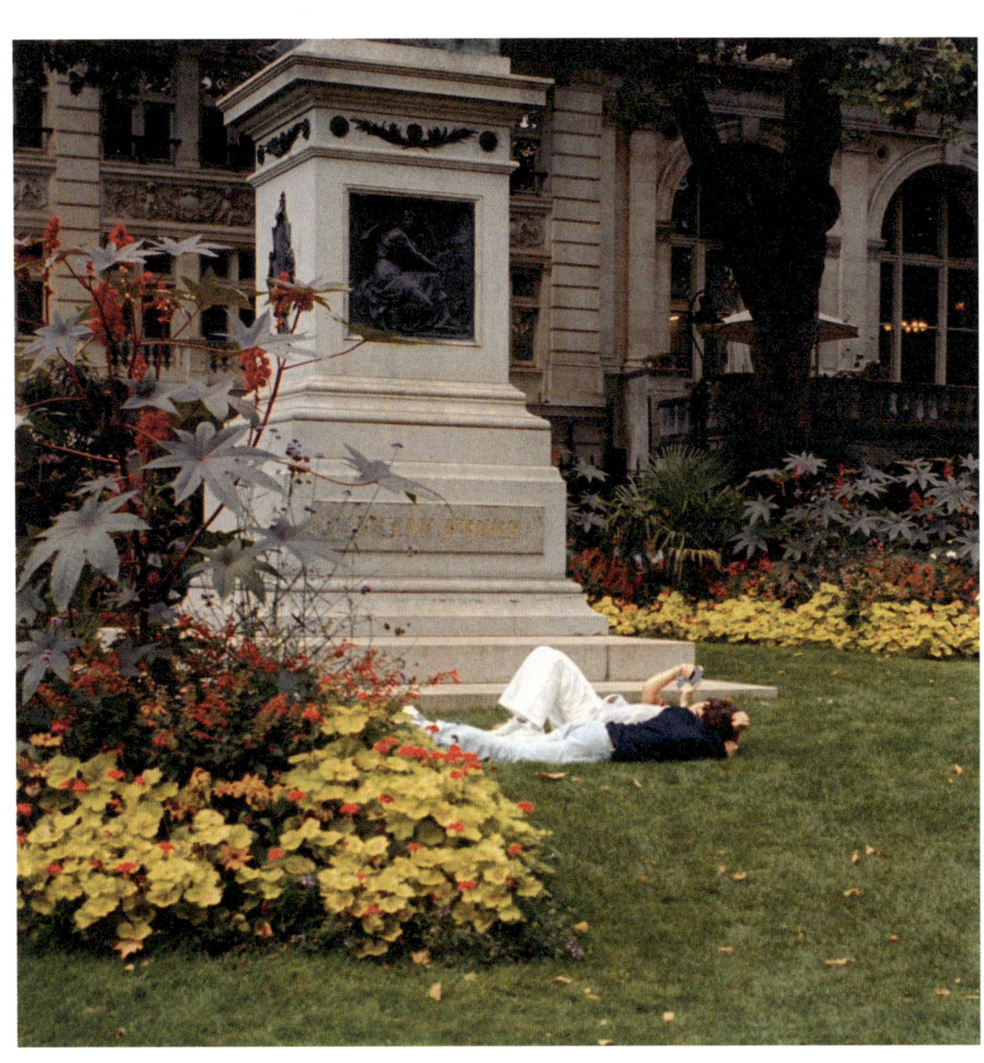

EVERY SEASON IS OURS

I think of the time when we were young and unable to be together, to feel one another safely, and to even look at each other. I think of oaths—the lives we promised one another the day we could entwine, a tight knot pulled at both ends over and over. I told you on a rainy July night that I believed, past the falling autumn leaves and the East Coast snow and the always-budding spring, that every season would be ours. From earth and with earth, we stay unmoving.

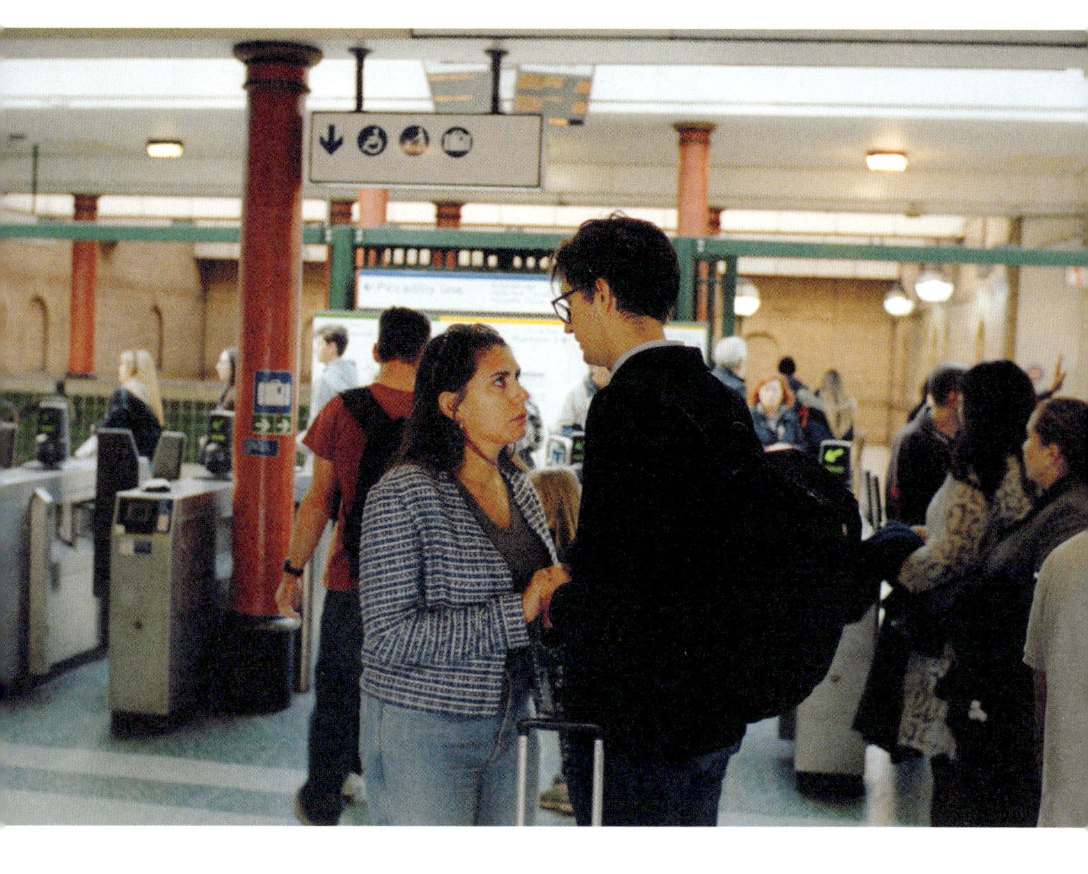
Piccadilly line

THE PAIN OF PAST LIVES

If I could take all the pain
your eyes hold and store it
in myself for lifetimes to come,

I would not hesitate.

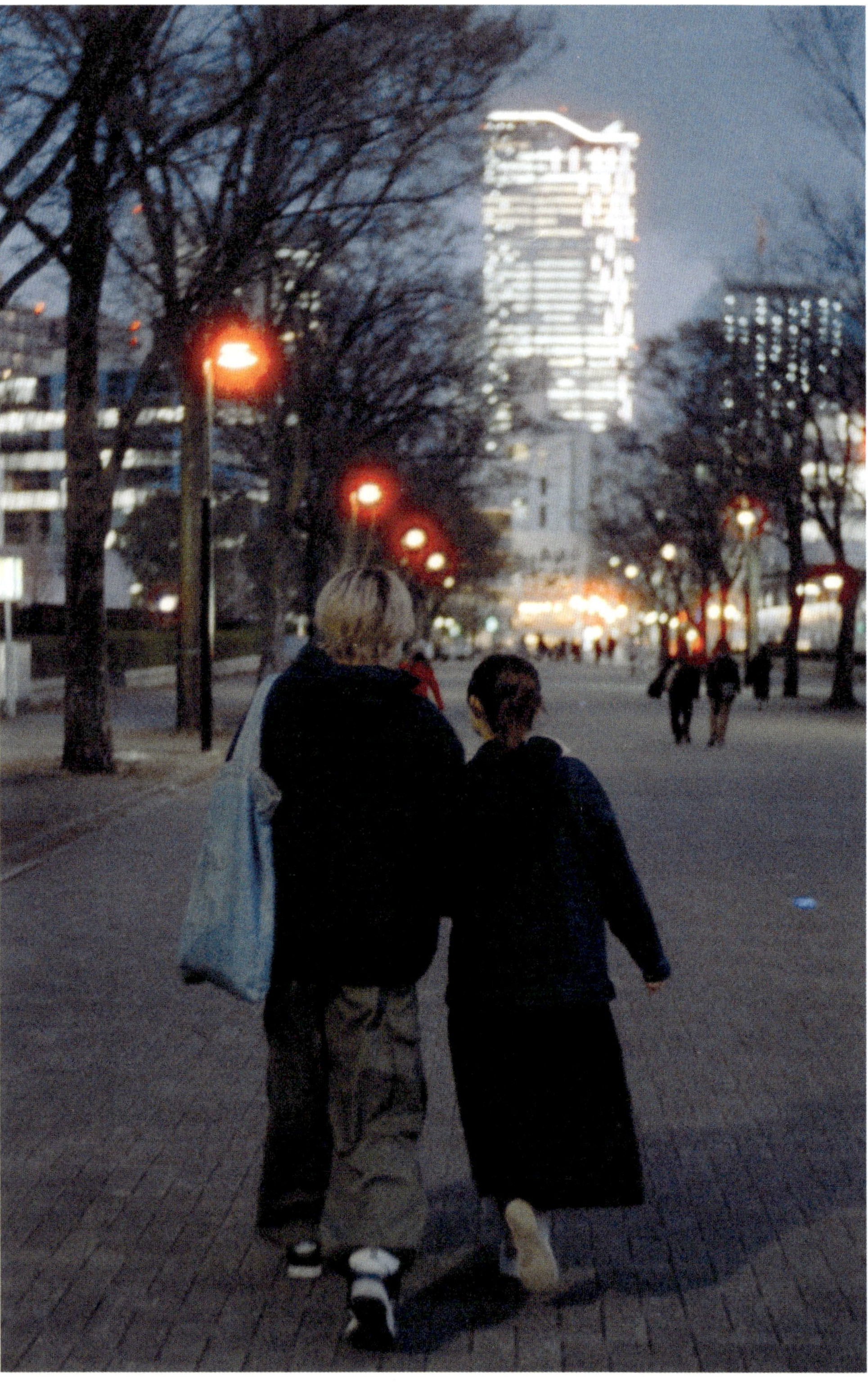

SHALL WE GO

home? Where

the morning birds sing. The wind there
dances across our bodies as if

it birthed us. Our heads lay
in the grass and our
eyes gaze at cloudless skies.

Solace, it's there. We knew,
we've always known.

AN ACT OF LOVE ITSELF

The most unnerving parts of endearing moments being held captive from me was knowing how unnatural those moments began to feel when they happened. Love felt distant, boxed away deep under clutter, in storage rooms we were told not to go into. I spent years searching for what I thought did not exist, only to find it in new people, new areas of life. That searching was love thriving. I look in the mirror and see how much more I need to be filled in, and know I can be.

LEAVING REMNANTS

Whenever you leave,
I begin to acknowledge the silence
in our home. You always take the joy we have built together
with you.

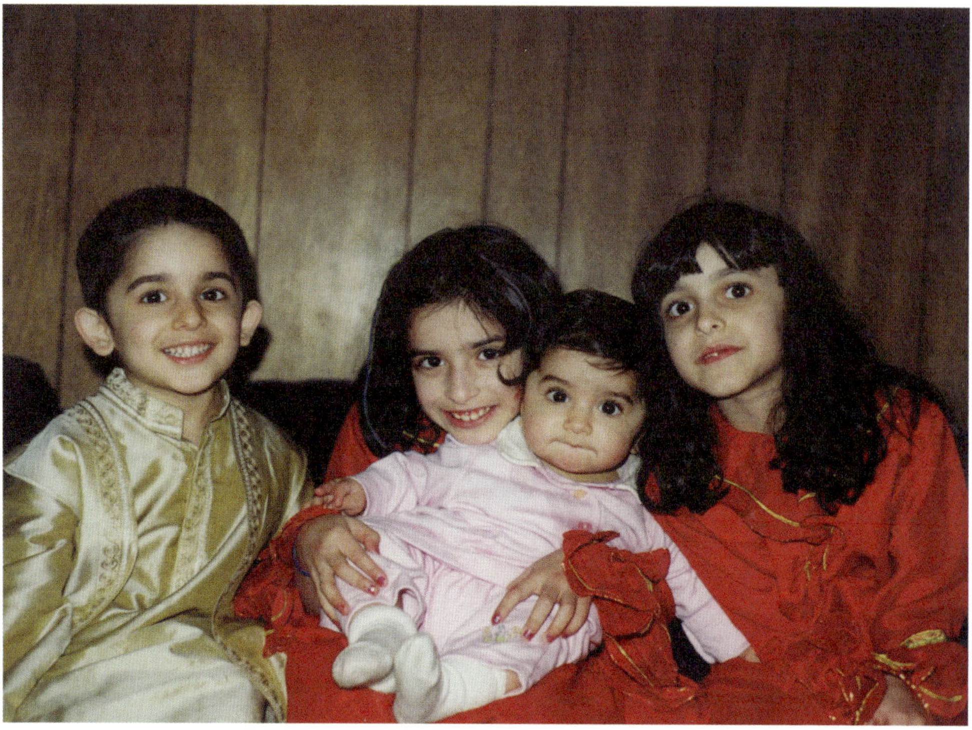

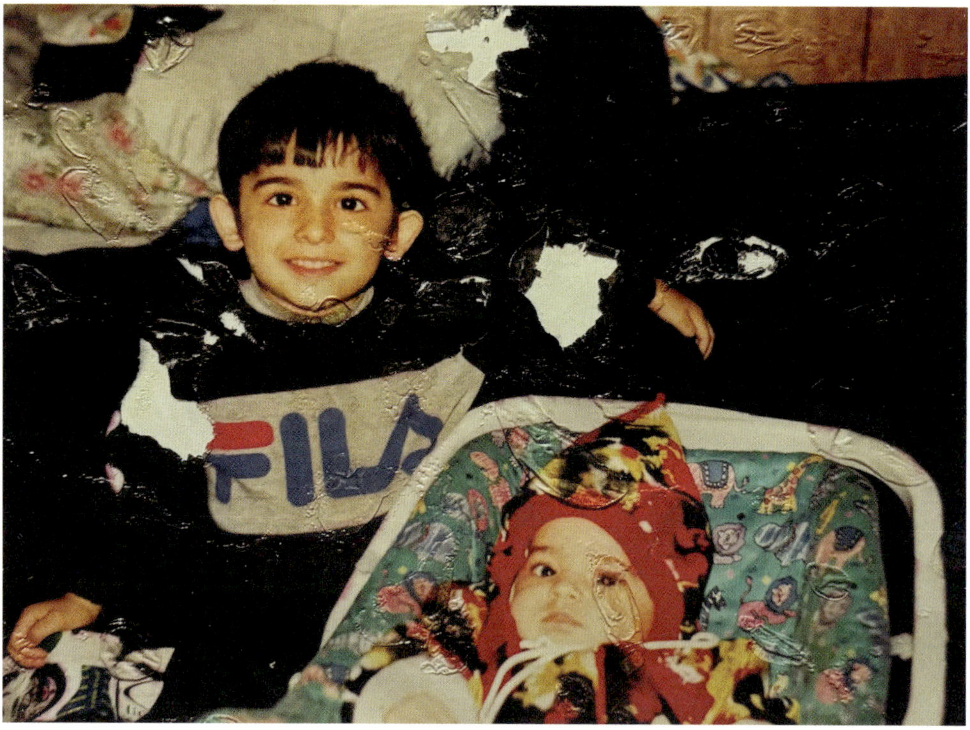

A.N.F.E.

A wire is attached
on my limbs, the same spots
as yours, and hers, and hers.
Nudging us toward
salvation.

ALWAYS HERE

In the sunlit park, you wrapped
your arms tight around my back,
whispering softly into my ears
that I belong. I ask where could I
possibly belong and you loosen
from me, telling me not to make it
complicated. *It's simple,* you say.
You belong here. Always here.

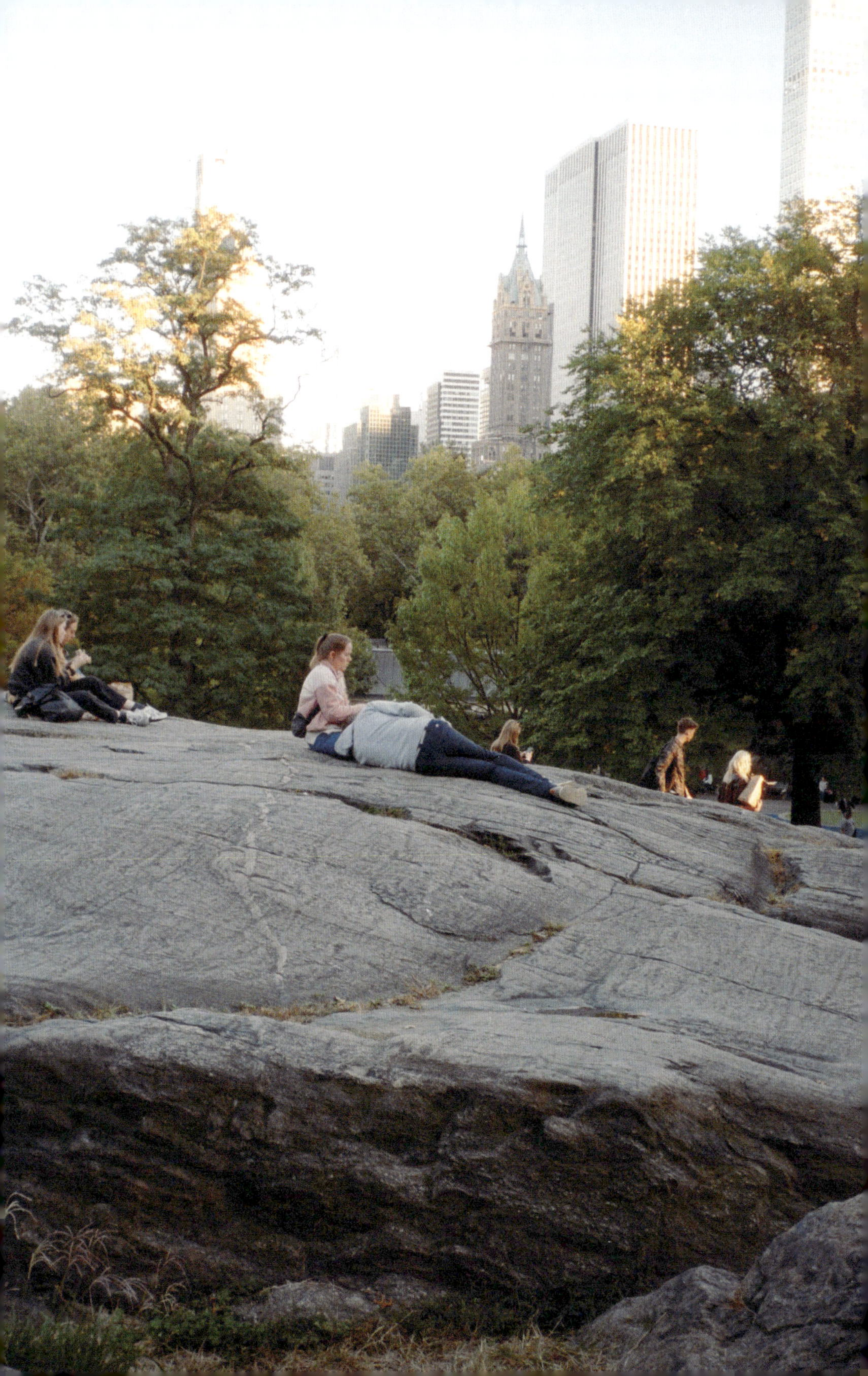

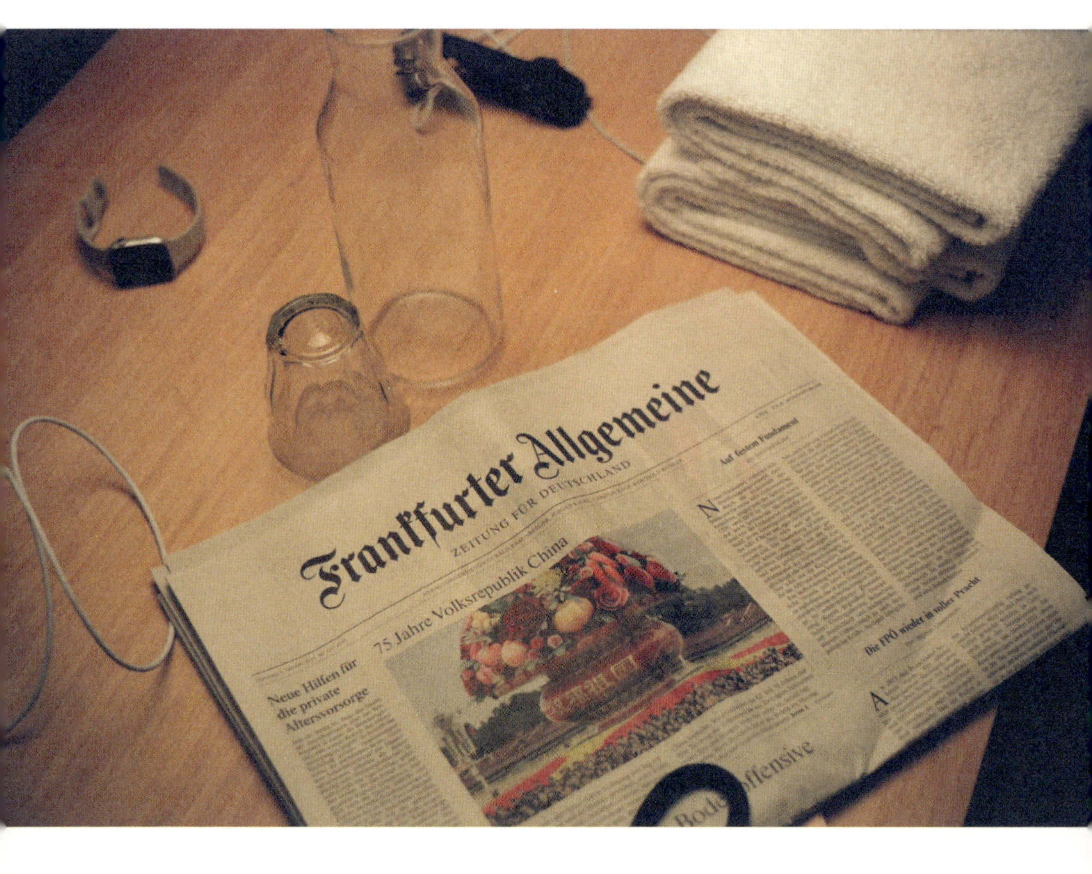
Frankfurter Allgemeine
ZEITUNG FÜR DEUTSCHLAND
75 Jahre Volksrepublik China
Neue Hilfen für die private Altersvorsorge
Die FPÖ wieder in voller Pracht

INSTANT RAMEN

In a hotel room halfway
across the world, we watch a romcom and pretend
life outside does not exist. We left it all
at the front door with our shoes, the coats
draped over hangers.
Your knees touch mine. Steam caresses your mouth
and fogs my glasses.

I tell myself, despite us being halfway across the world,

instant ramen will always taste exactly
the same.

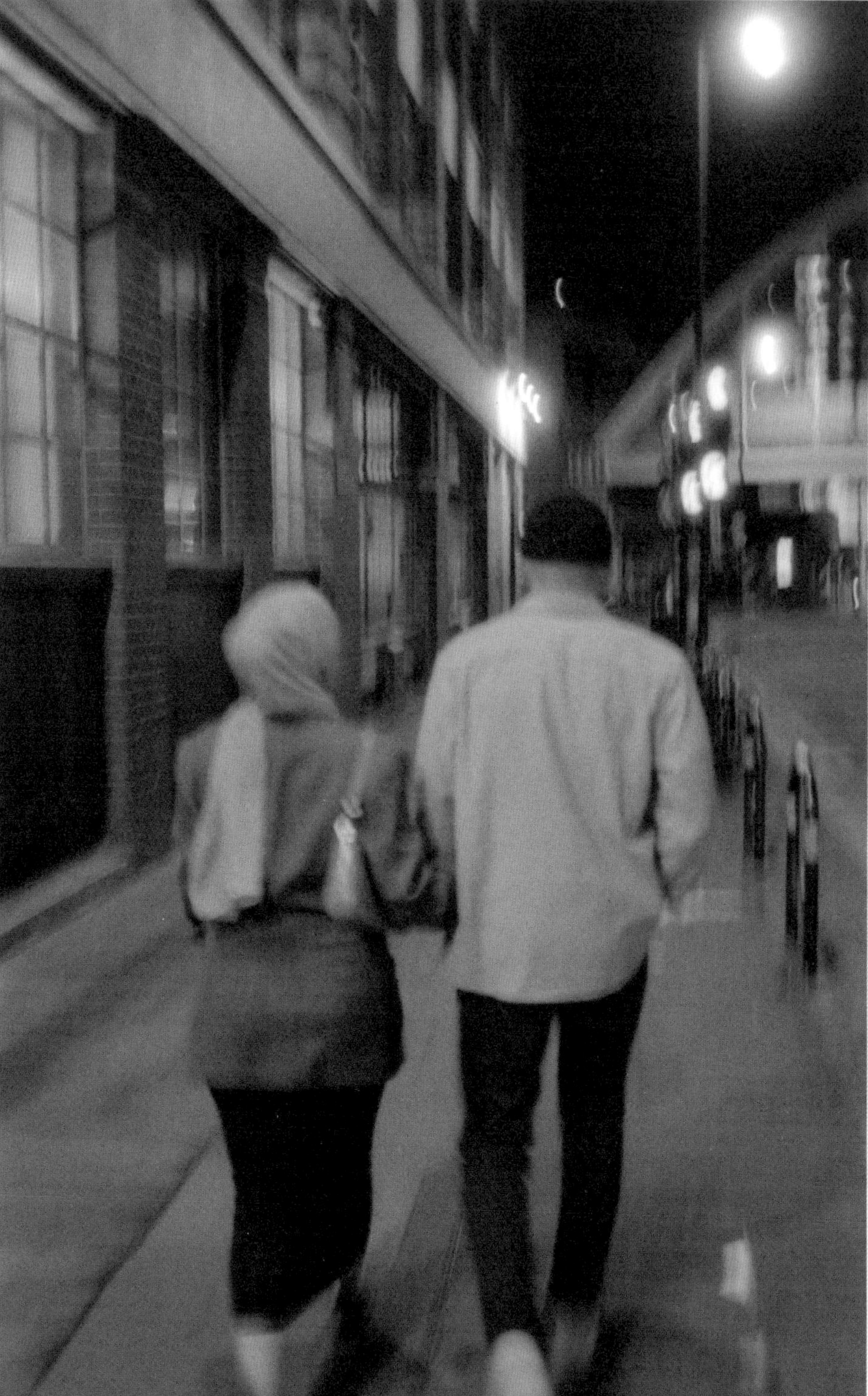

OPEN YOUR HEART

Leave your soul vast
and welcoming, for there is so much
love here, and I need you
to receive it.

CARVED INTO ANOTHER

Even on the days when you are
nowhere near me, I feel the love
we have carved into one another,
as if we were a bench in a nature-
filled park. No matter the distance,

I know we are permanent and give
one another a place to rest.

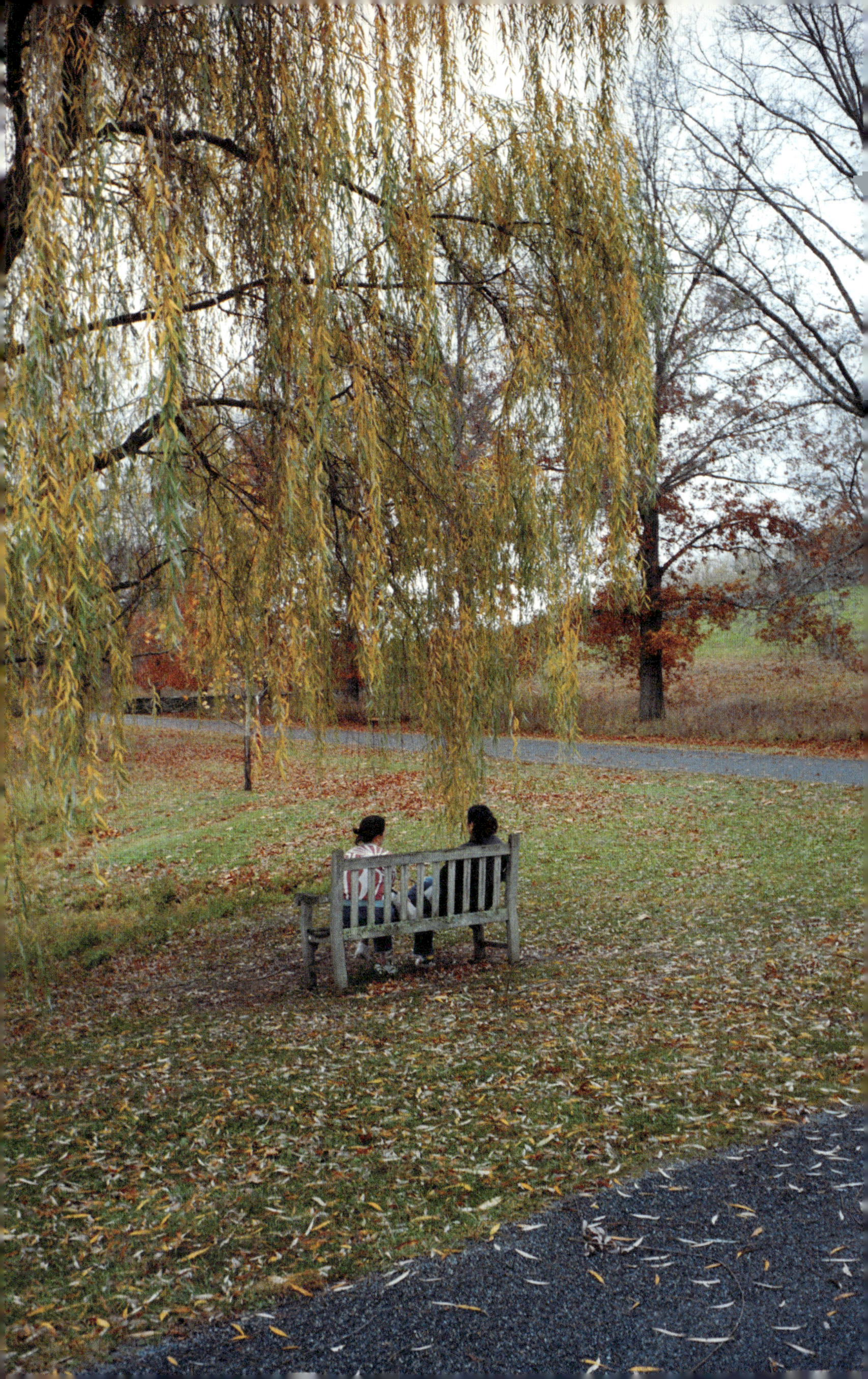

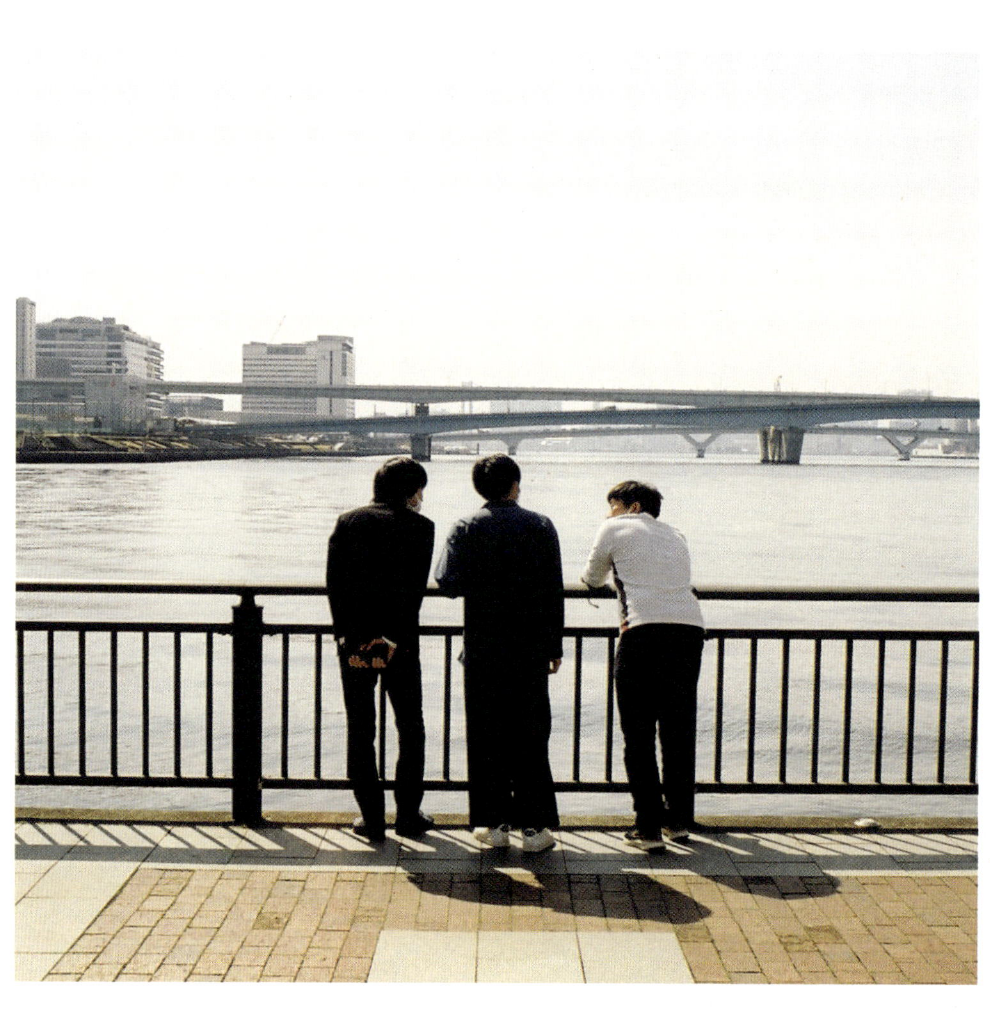

EVER SINCE WE WERE YOUNG,

we've promised each other to remain
unchanged. To be the same kids we were
when we fell in love. Love is also that,

isn't it? Friendship that lives if you allow
its breathing. Its watering. Even after
so many years, us growing—we aren't six

anymore but our roots have wrapped around
each other, pulling us closer.
As if we're branches, tightening into thick knots.
Even if the land beneath us

breaks open, we'll fall together,
together. Our souls share history,
this harmony we cannot find elsewhere.

I CARRY YOU

I observe you
in every inch of this world.
From hydrangeas and sunflowers
at the grocery store, to
your favorite books
on shelves, and the notepad
you love to use. You've left parts
of yourself everywhere
I look, and I carry
those pieces in me.

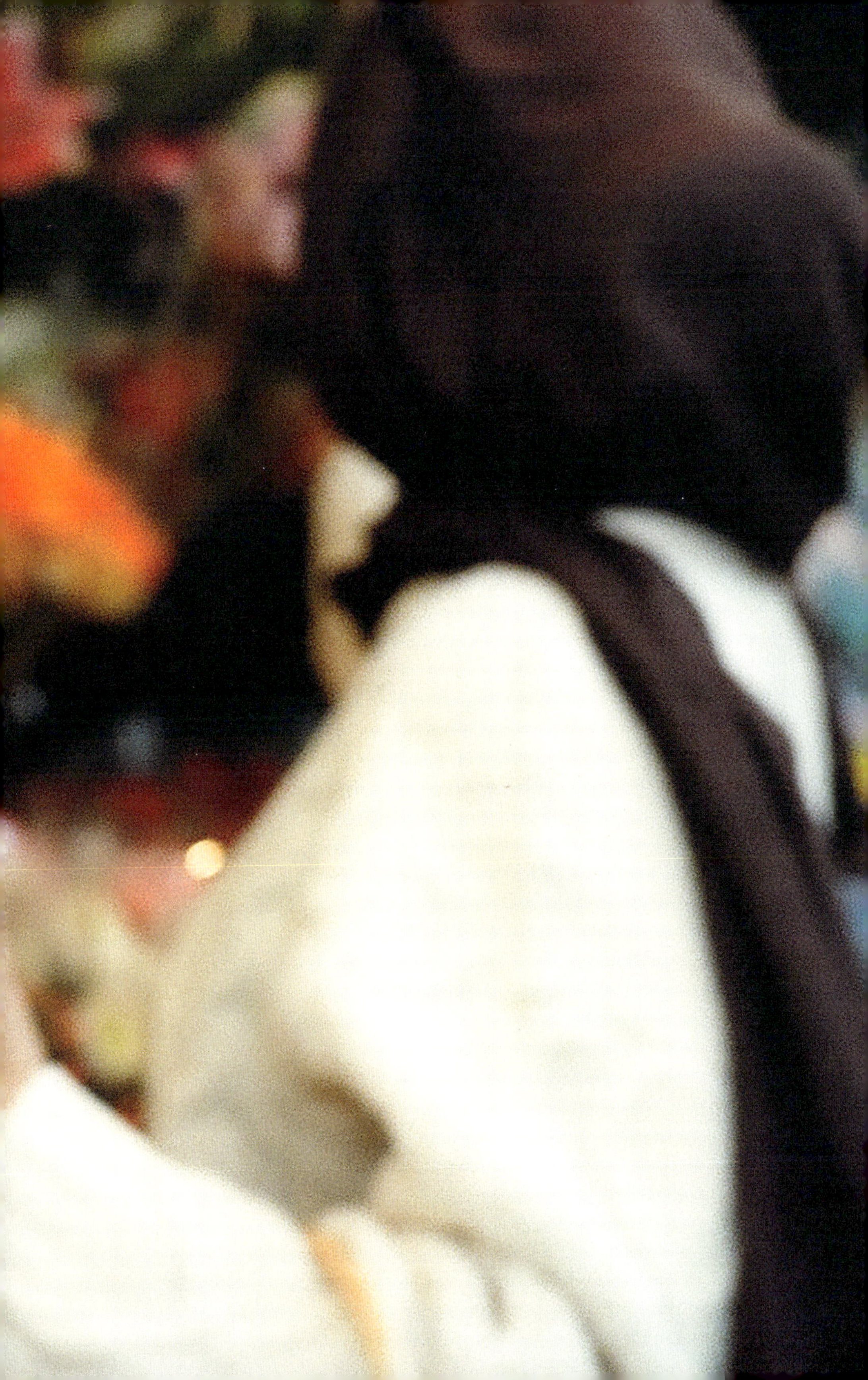

Isn't it nice? To be
cherished so tenderly,
so simply.
As if your soul was
destined for it.

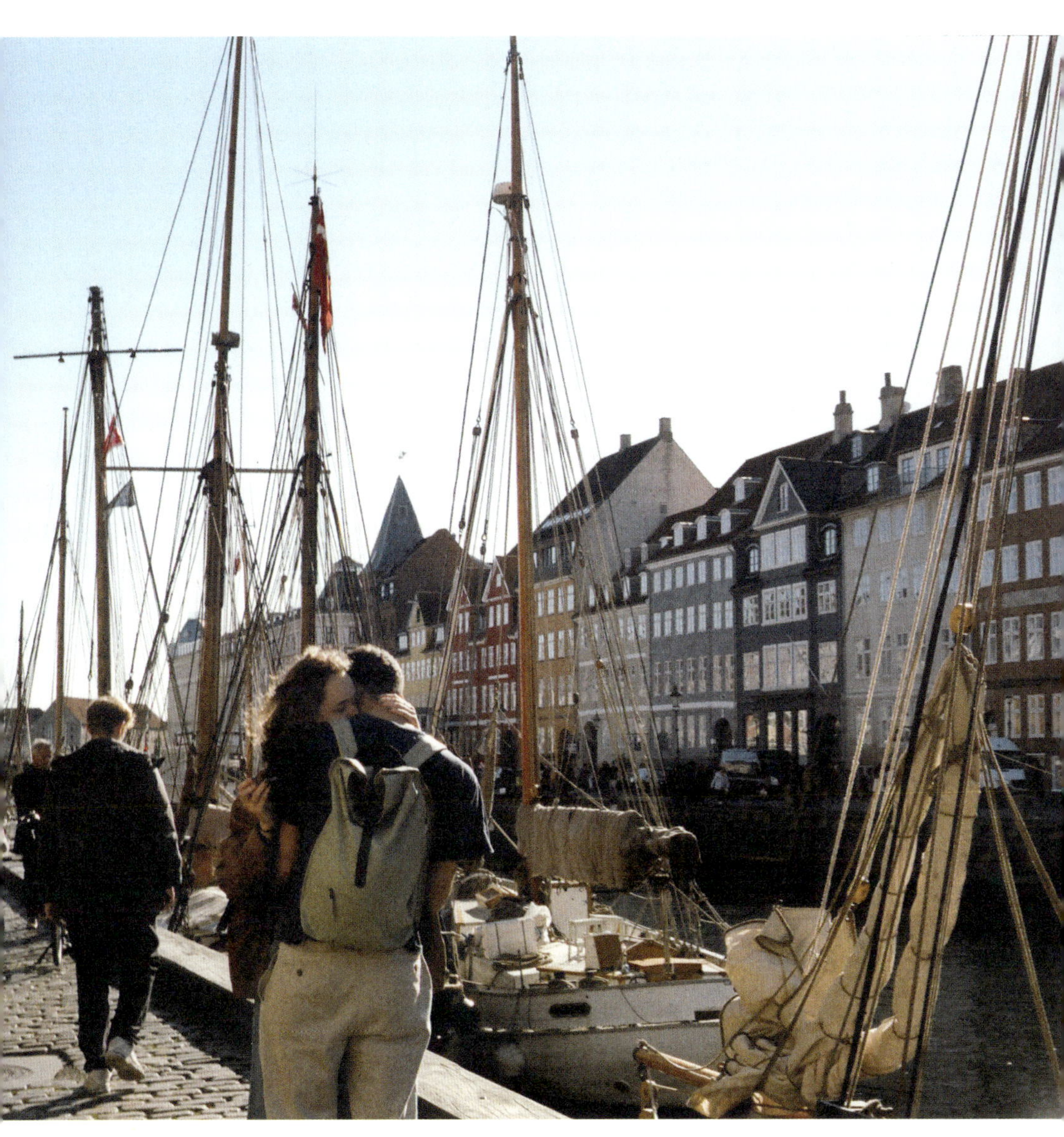

TO FEEL ALL OF YOU

I wish I were cool water
streaming through your veins.
What a blessing it must be
to feel you in your entirety.

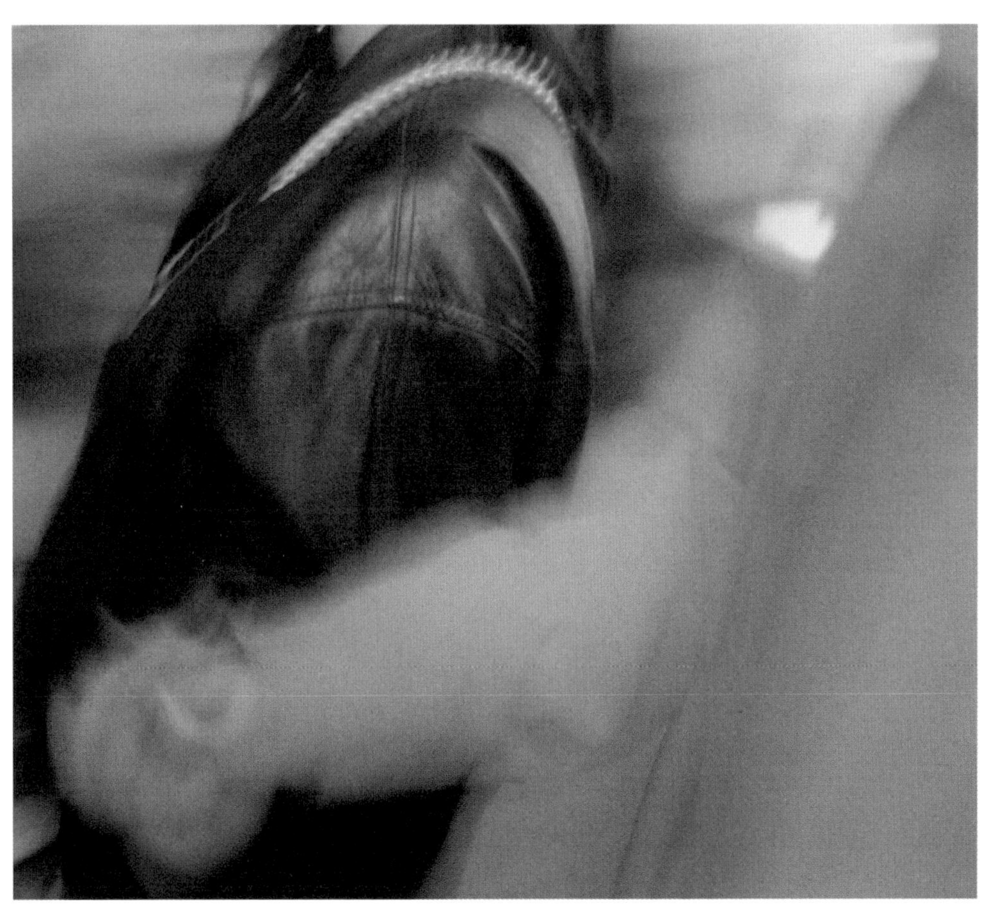

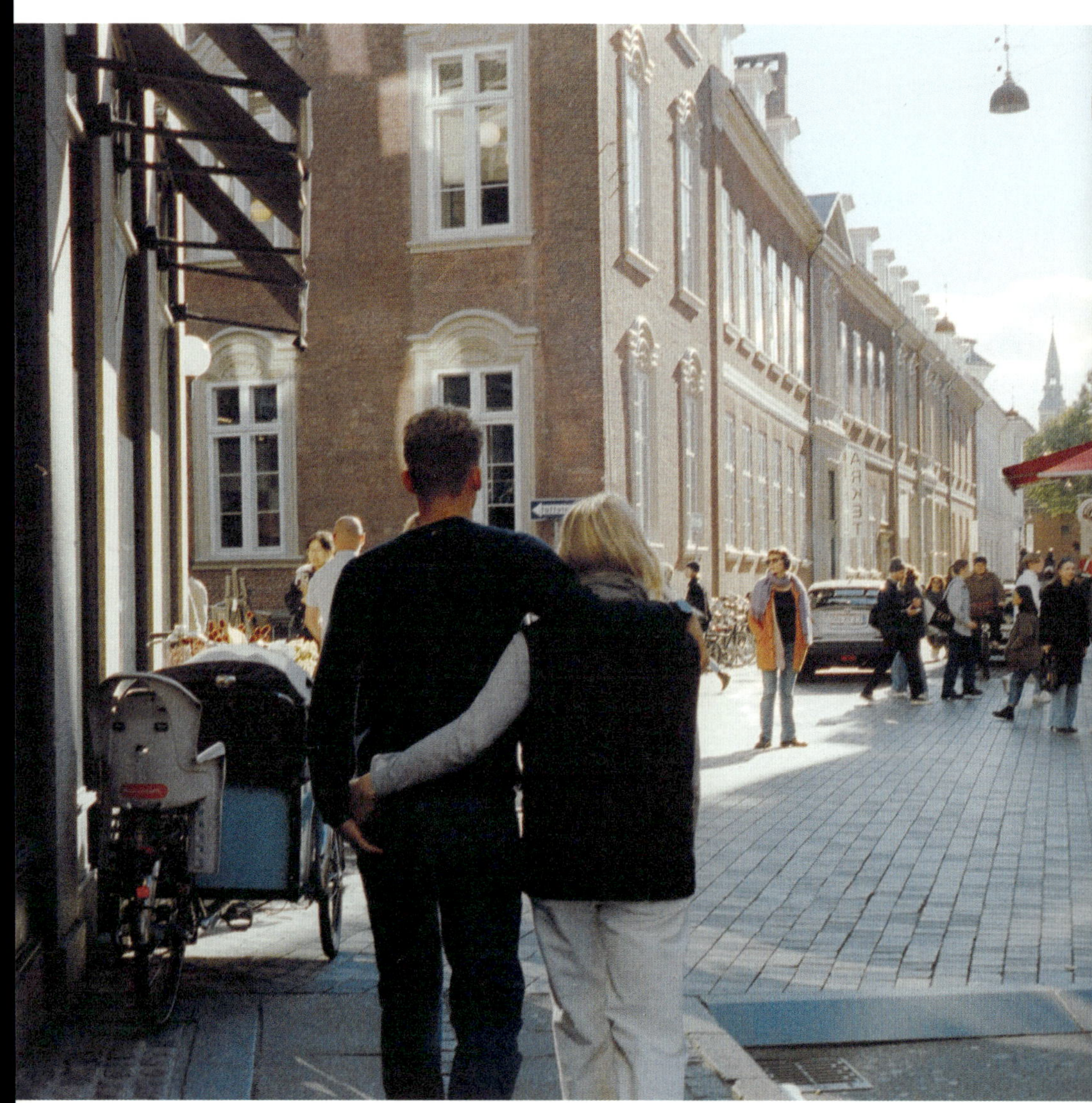

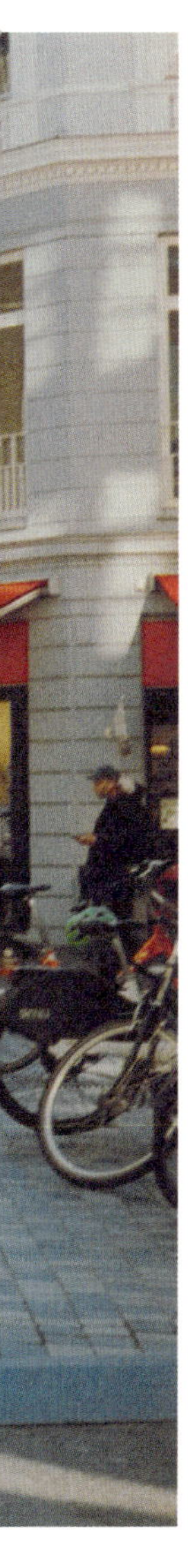

TO BE

Leaves snap beneath our feet next
to a blood-red corvette begging to be

bought. Apple orchards hang low,
cider donuts we delight in

as the season ends, the days shorter
and the sun drowsy. Skyscrapers

do not shift colors like autumn trees,
which is why we're here, you tell me

as we lay sprawled together. Donuts
in the fridge, large Honeycrisps spilling

out onto the table. Don't you agree?
The window is cracked ever so slightly

behind a melody of morning birds,
I can't find myself anywhere else I'd like

to be.

SUMMER, 2025

If all of our Augusts
are spent looking at fiery skies,
salt-coated lips,
your hands intertwined with mine,

I would not mind an eternity of warmth.

BEFORE YOU/AFTER YOU

On the nights without you,
restlessness would give me a squeeze—
my eyelids light as floating feathers,
my bed a thousand nails prickling me.

I find it odd—how easily I could live not knowing you.
How my days without you now are incomplete,
like the sun shaded every second by deep clouds.

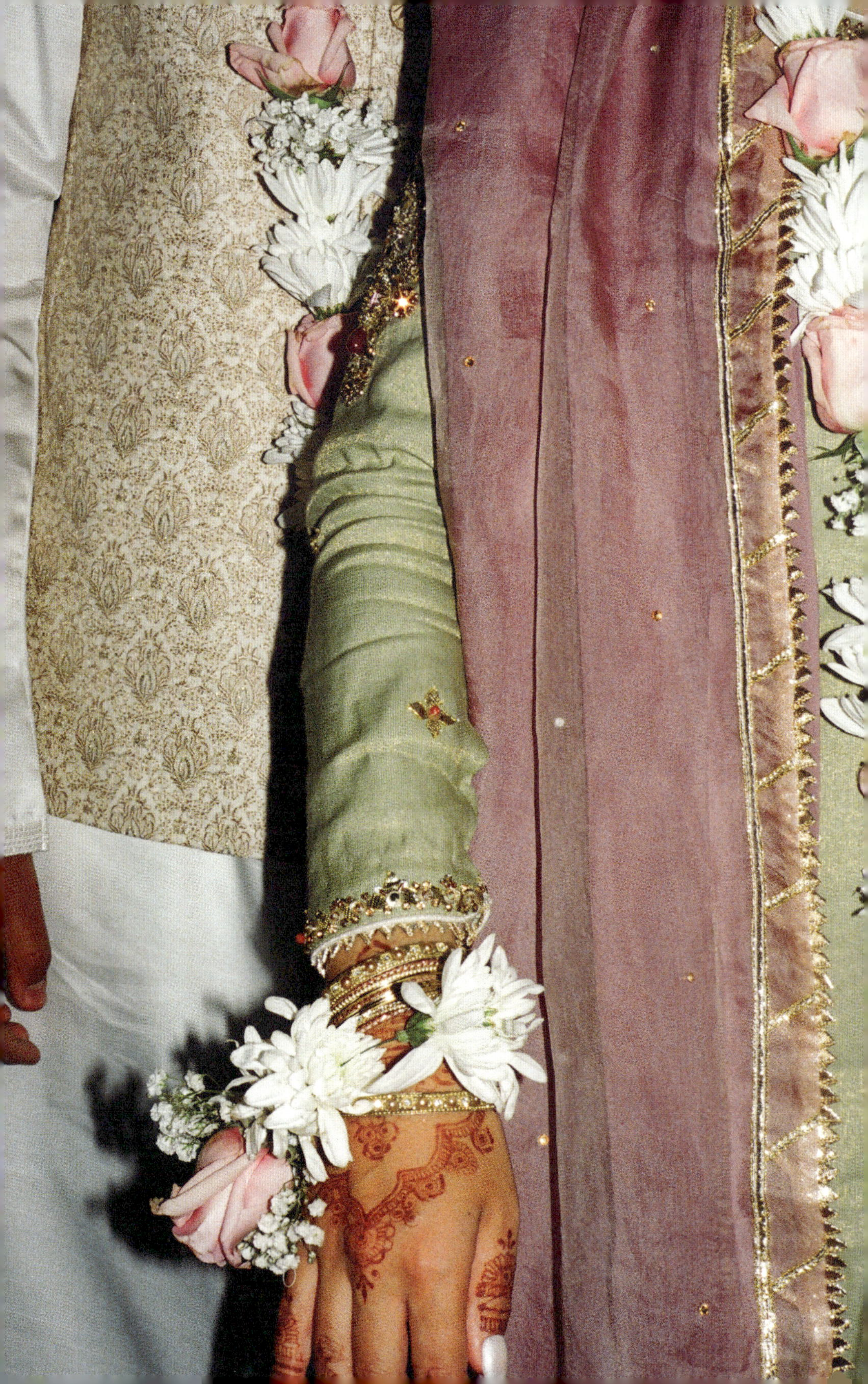

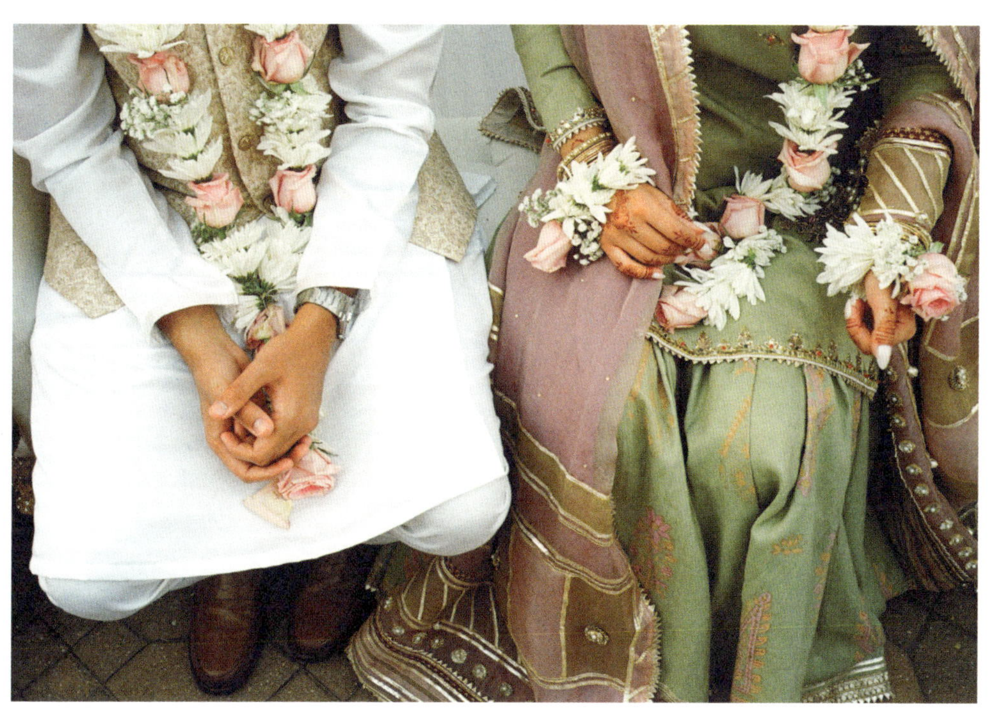

I GIVE TO YOU TO GIVE TO MYSELF

I have given you more than I have given myself,
and while it frightens me—

I know that my desire for you is the only way
the love in me can smile.

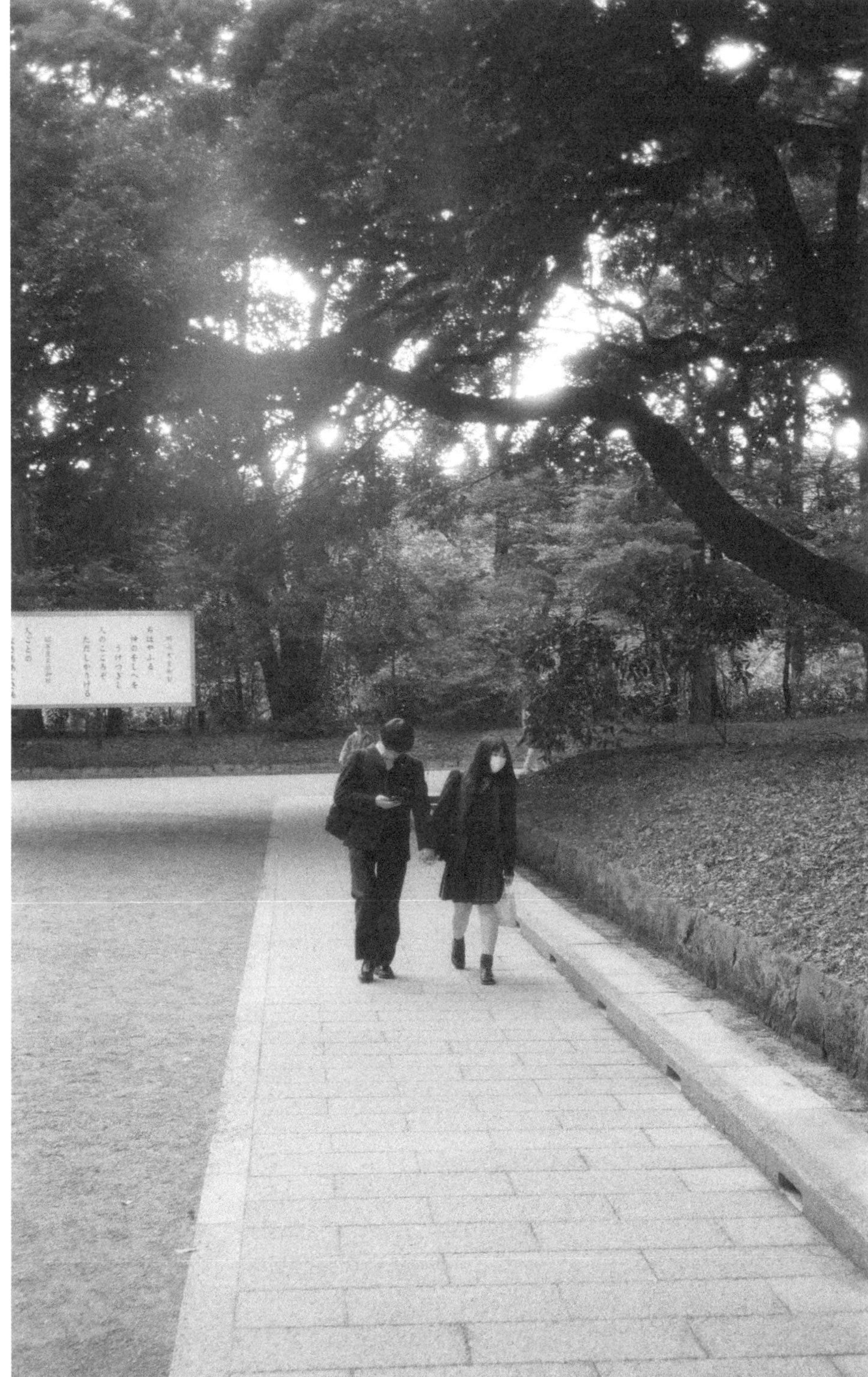

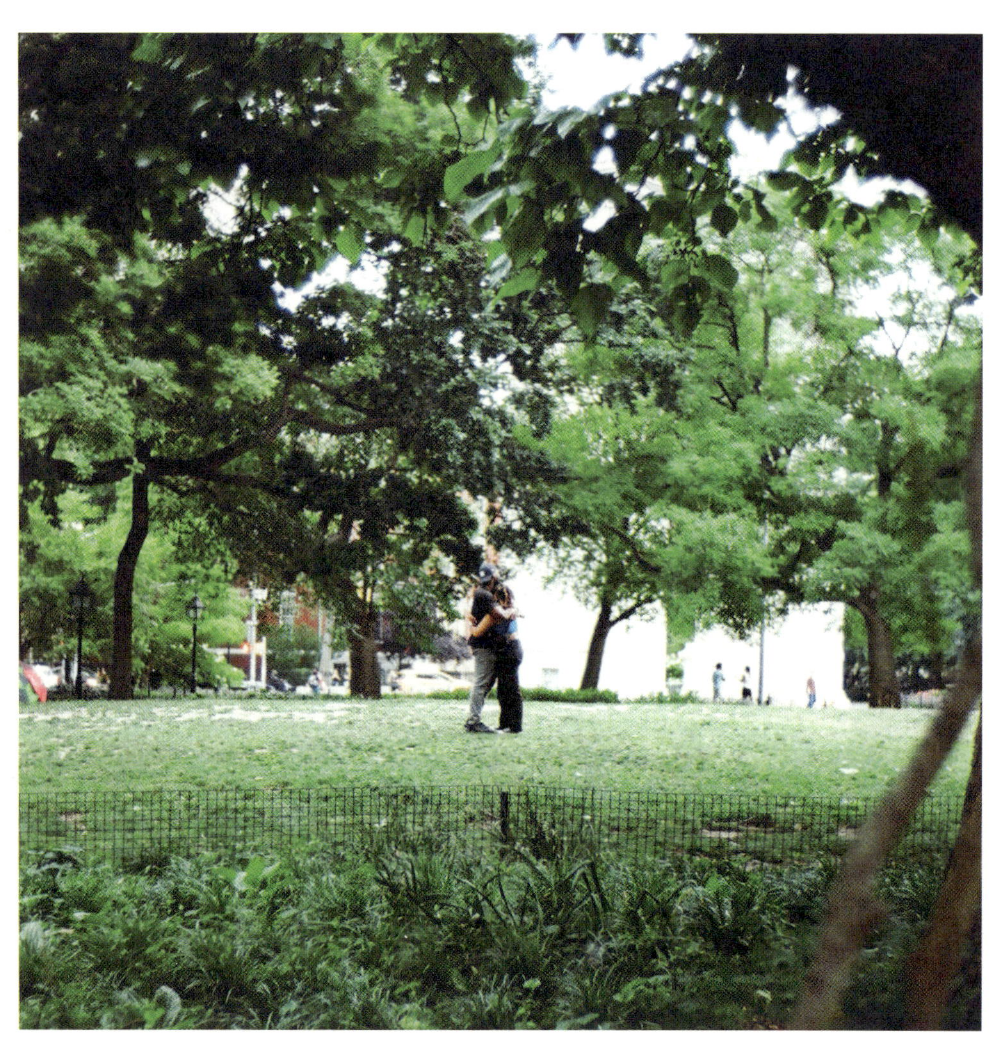

REFORMATION

You may not recognize me
at times, like a tree going through
its early trimmings, but I'd like for you
to know that I am forever in the midst
of reform. That I will not be the same
tomorrow, and the tomorrows after.

But I hope it is good. I hope
the vibrancy is new, with limbs
long enough to meet
with embrace.

MET

It is said that one can find art
wherever they look—yet I have not
been able to find artistry

more meaningful than you.

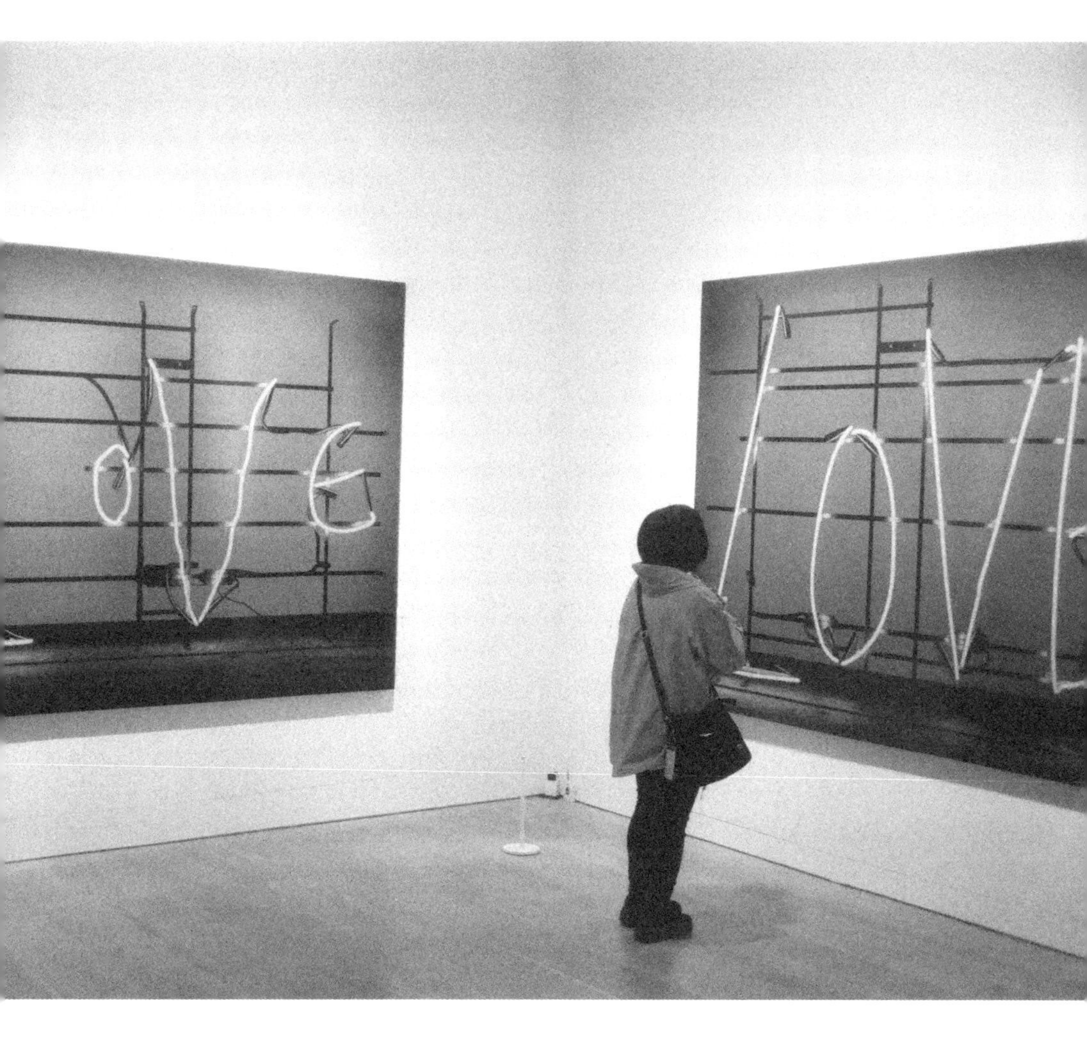

MORNINGS AND NIGHTS HOLD ON TO YOUR SOUL. I WILL ENJOY WITNESSING THE VERY GRACE THESE DAYS CARRY.

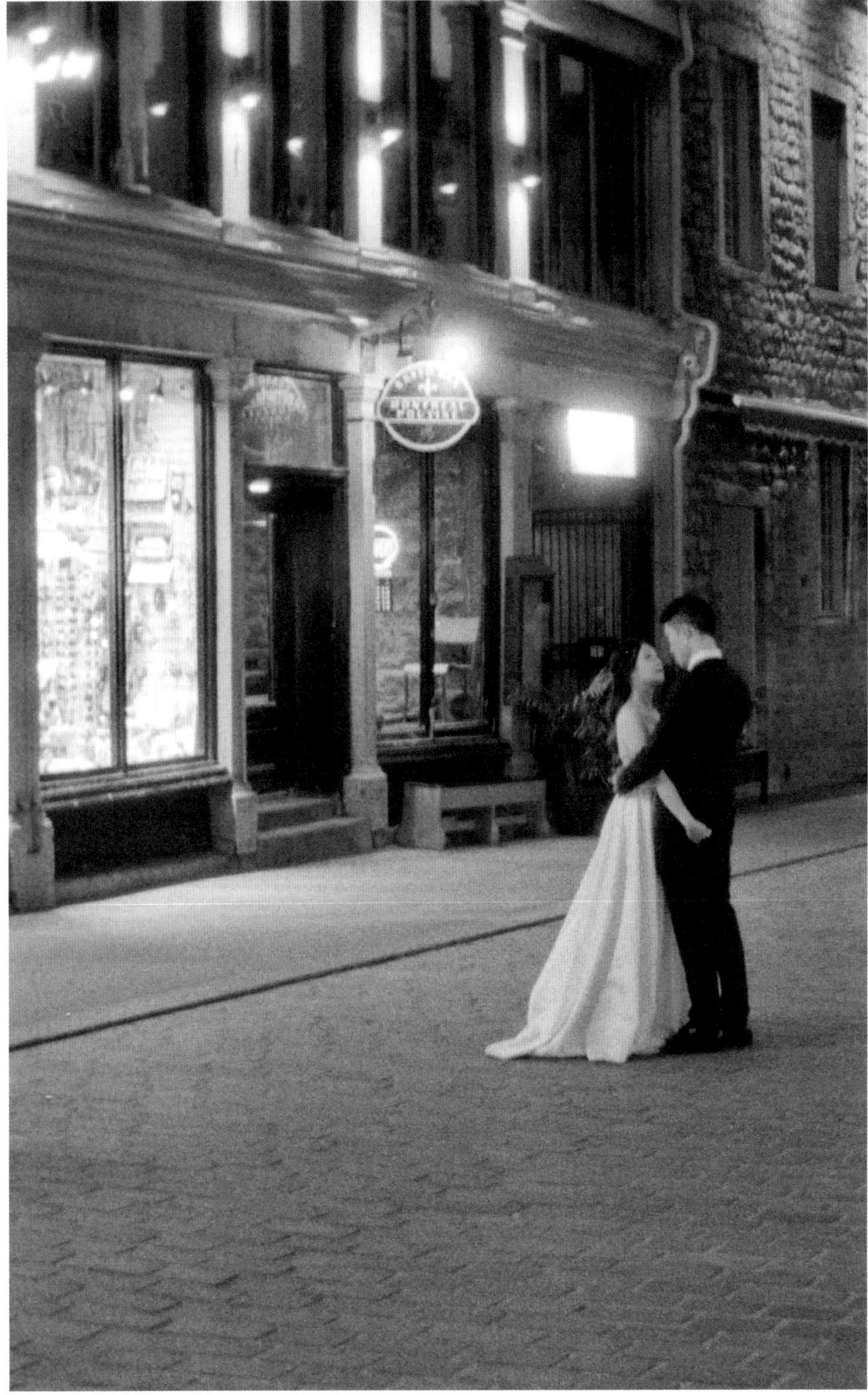

I DREAM

of the days when life
grabs hold of me and begs
me to accept how tender
the world can be. All of life's
carryings being able to fit
in between the gaps of my ribs.

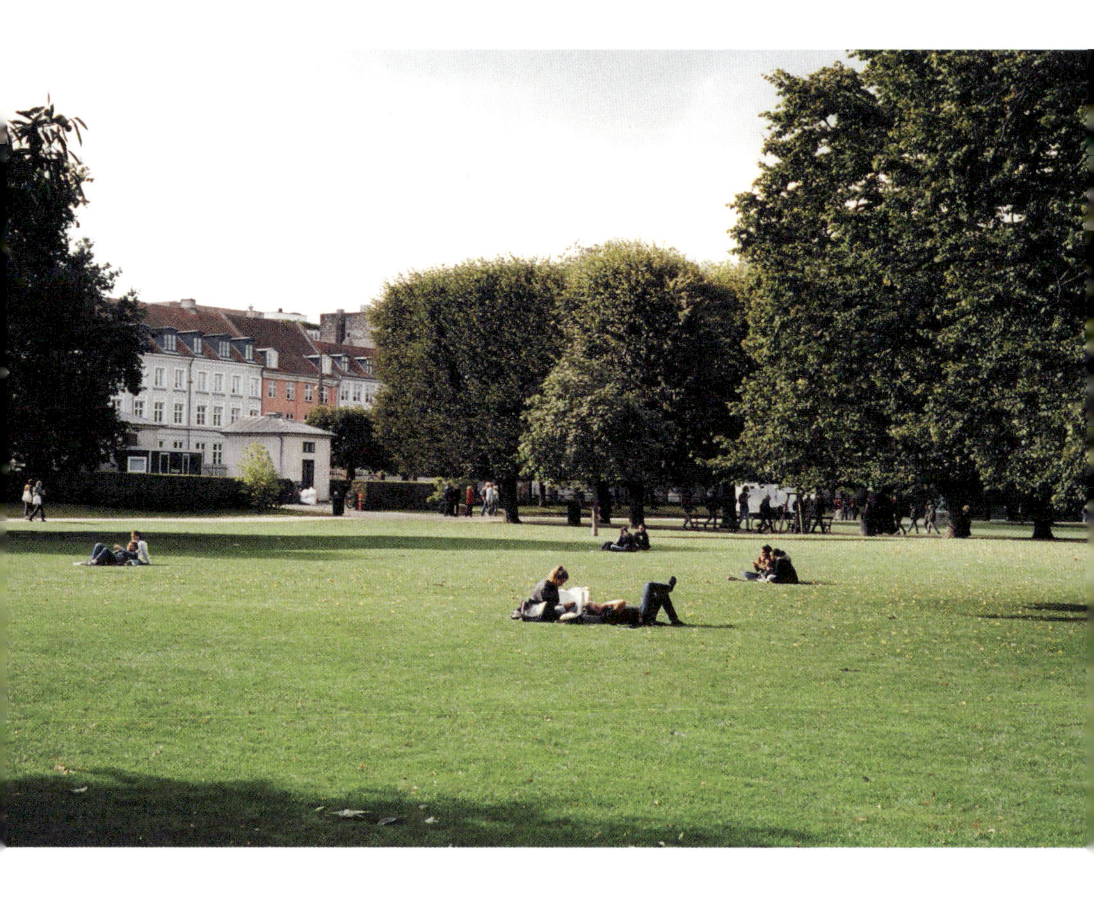

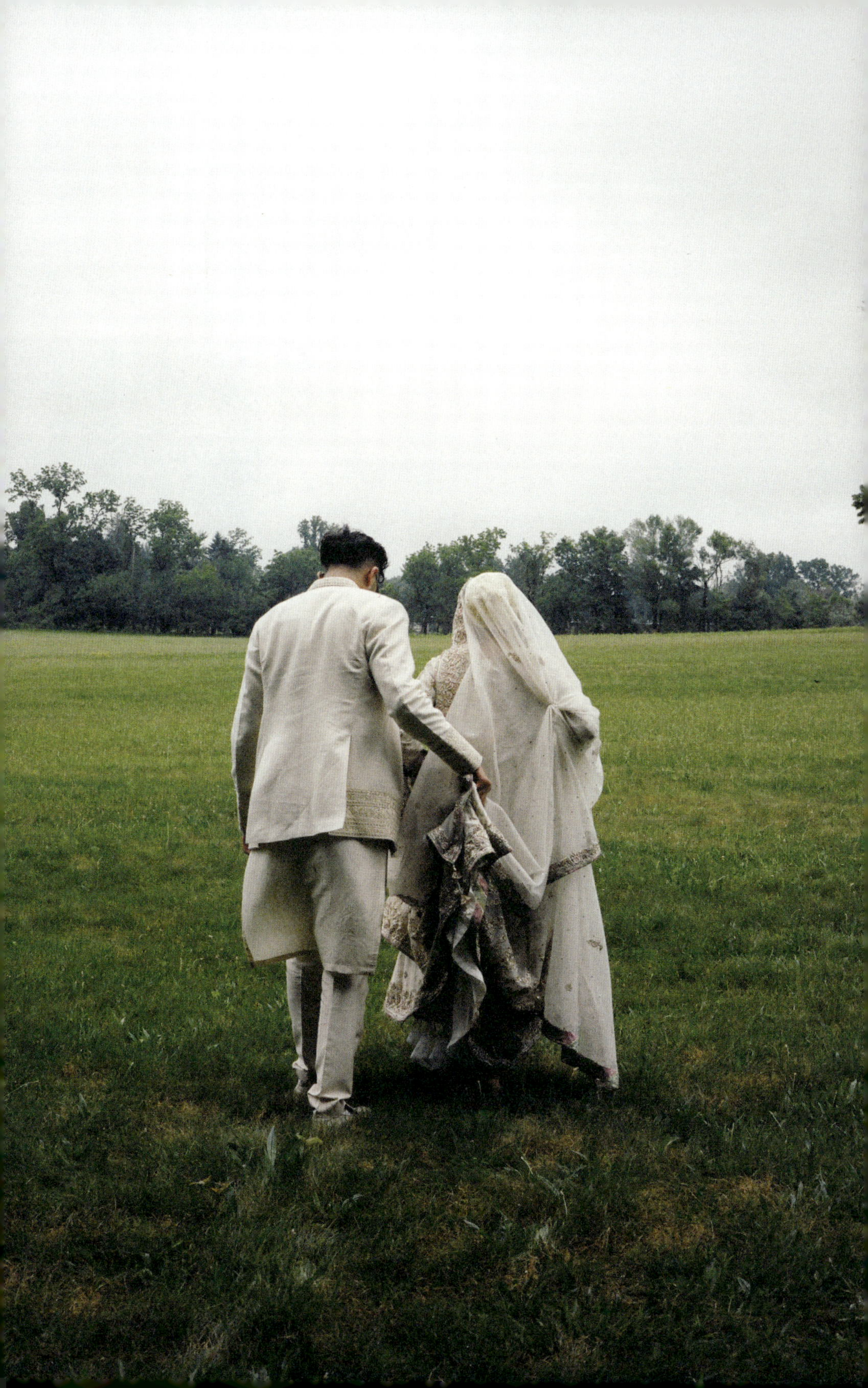

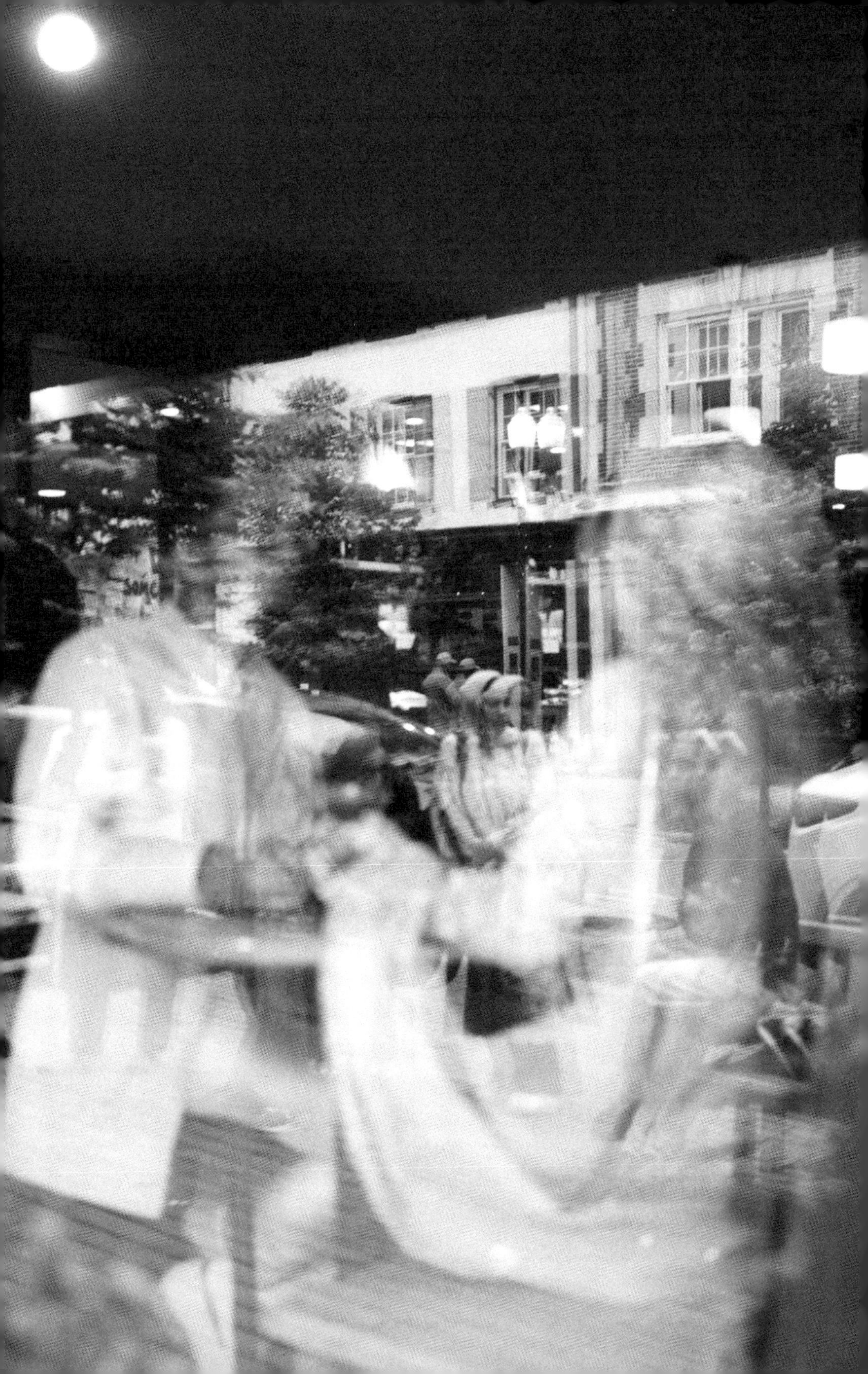

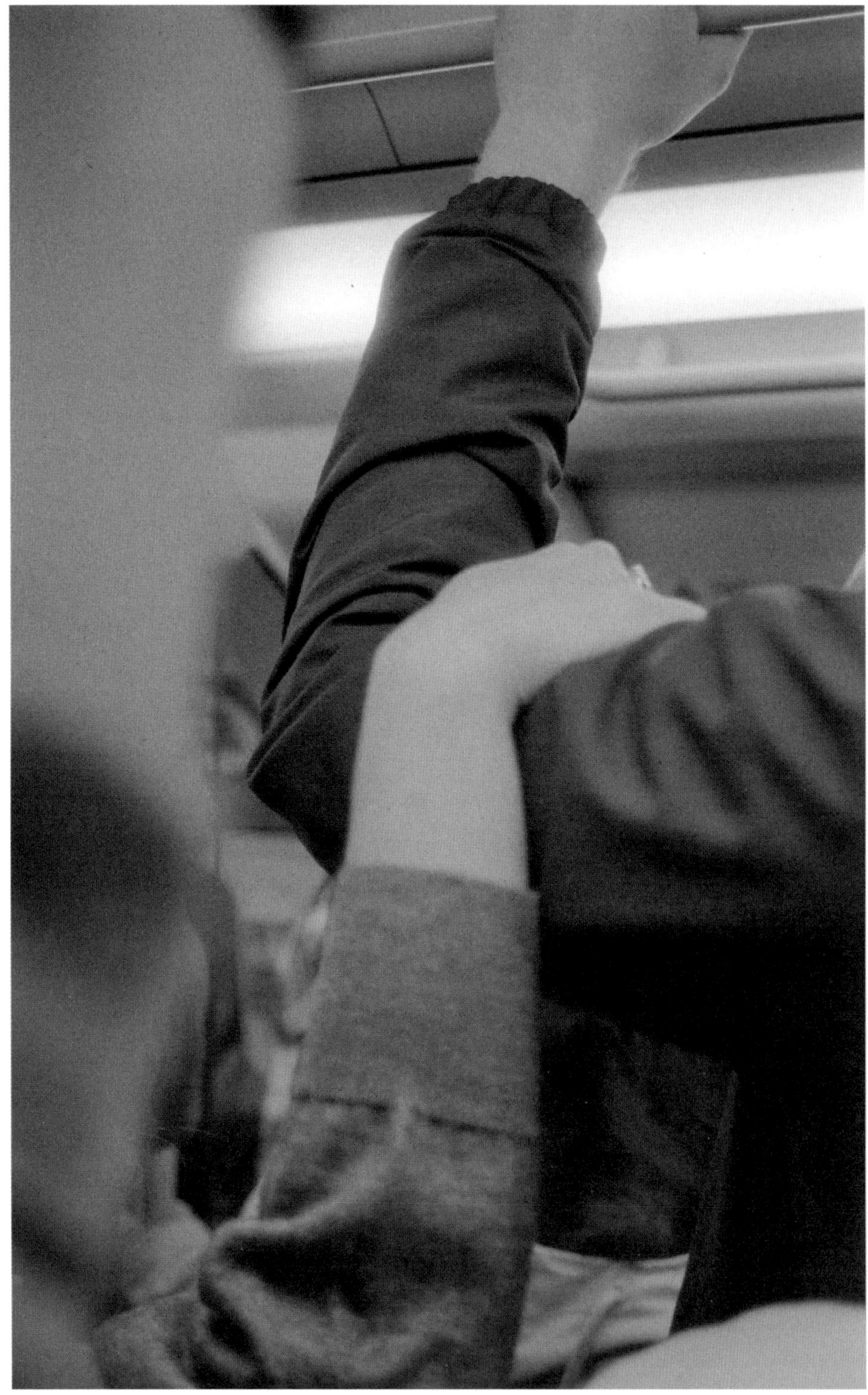

RELEARNING GRACE

You speak loving words to me,
words I once fled from.

I would sprint until my legs grew numb,
until the sheer weight of the words
crumbled my bones into fine, beachy sand.

When you speak now, my heart
remains still. I stand in the sand, my limbs
submerged, grace surrounding me.

STAR POLLUTION

Beneath the pure night sky, give me
one more look. One more kiss
before the orange hue greets us—the stars
glimmer the final moments we recall.

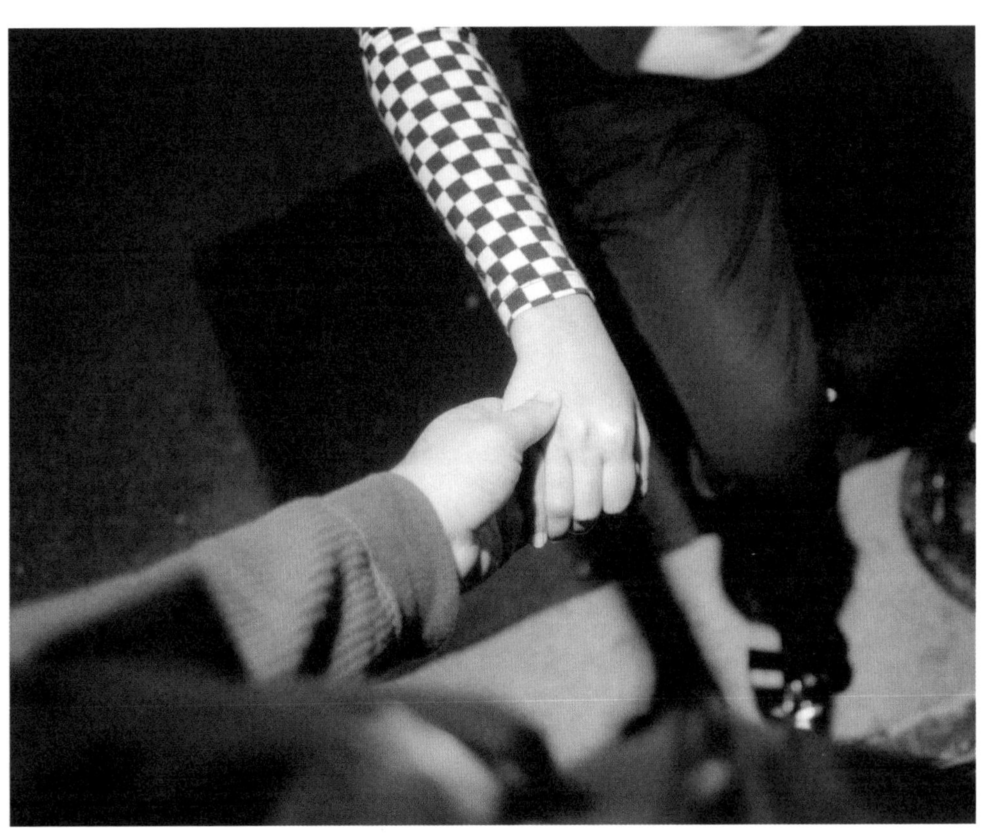

IN AN EMPTY THEATER

Days without you do not feel
like days, but memories passing
by me, projecting seconds we've spent
nurturing one another.

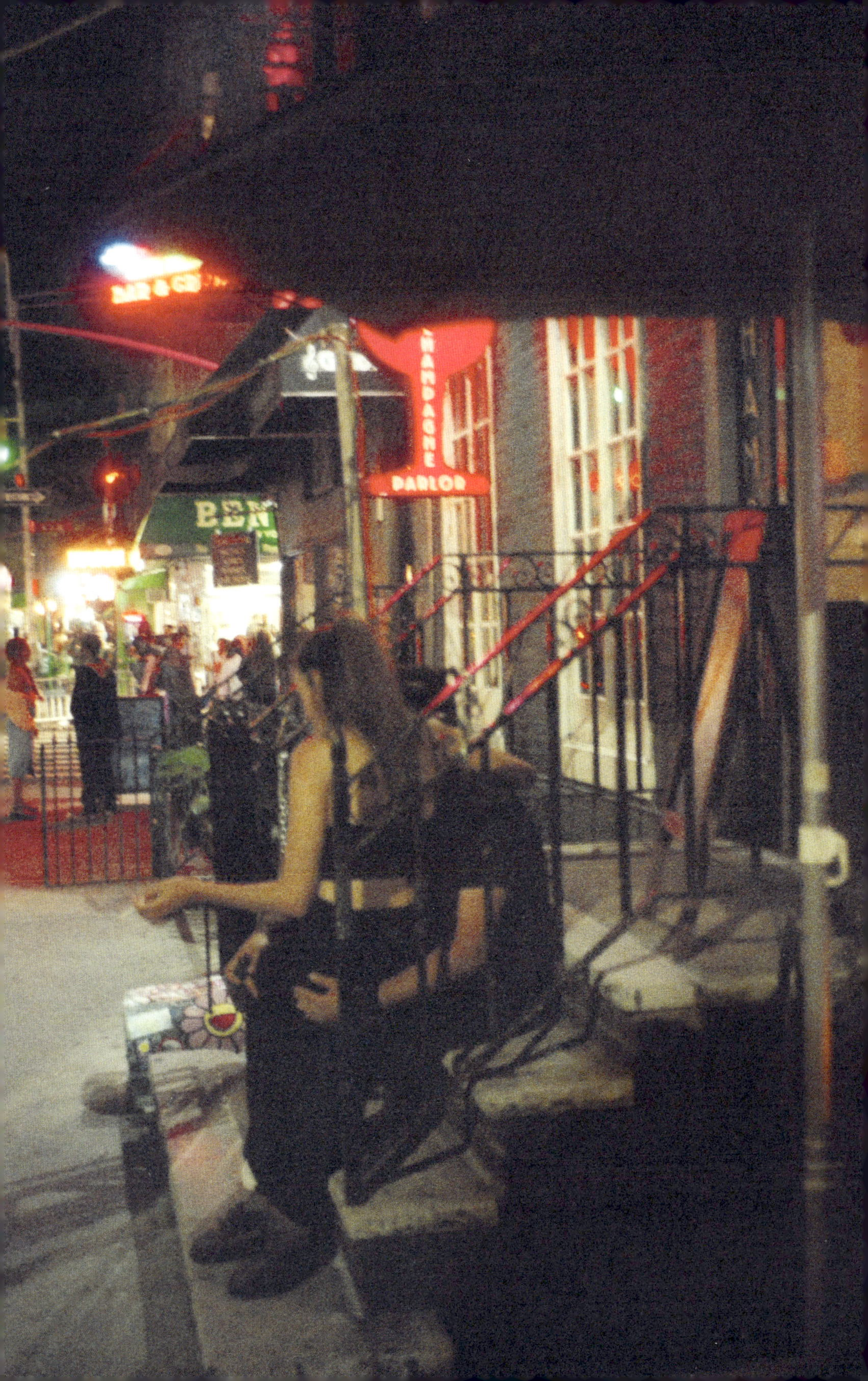

PARLOR
BEN

LATELY, I'VE BEEN PONDERING

the power of our love.
I've realized the many ways
our bond has changed
over the years. Adoration remains
in every waking moment—two of us learning
to become more of each other's refuge

we can continue to nourish
what we've already built.

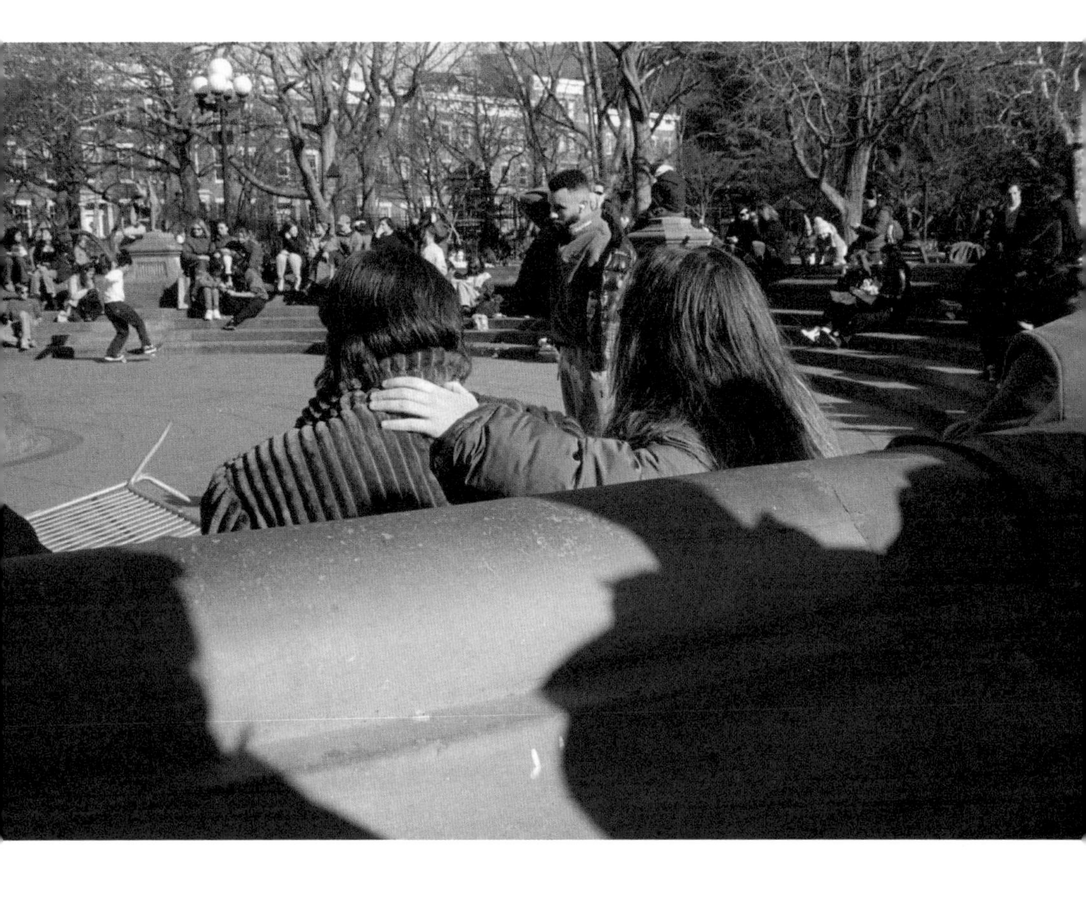

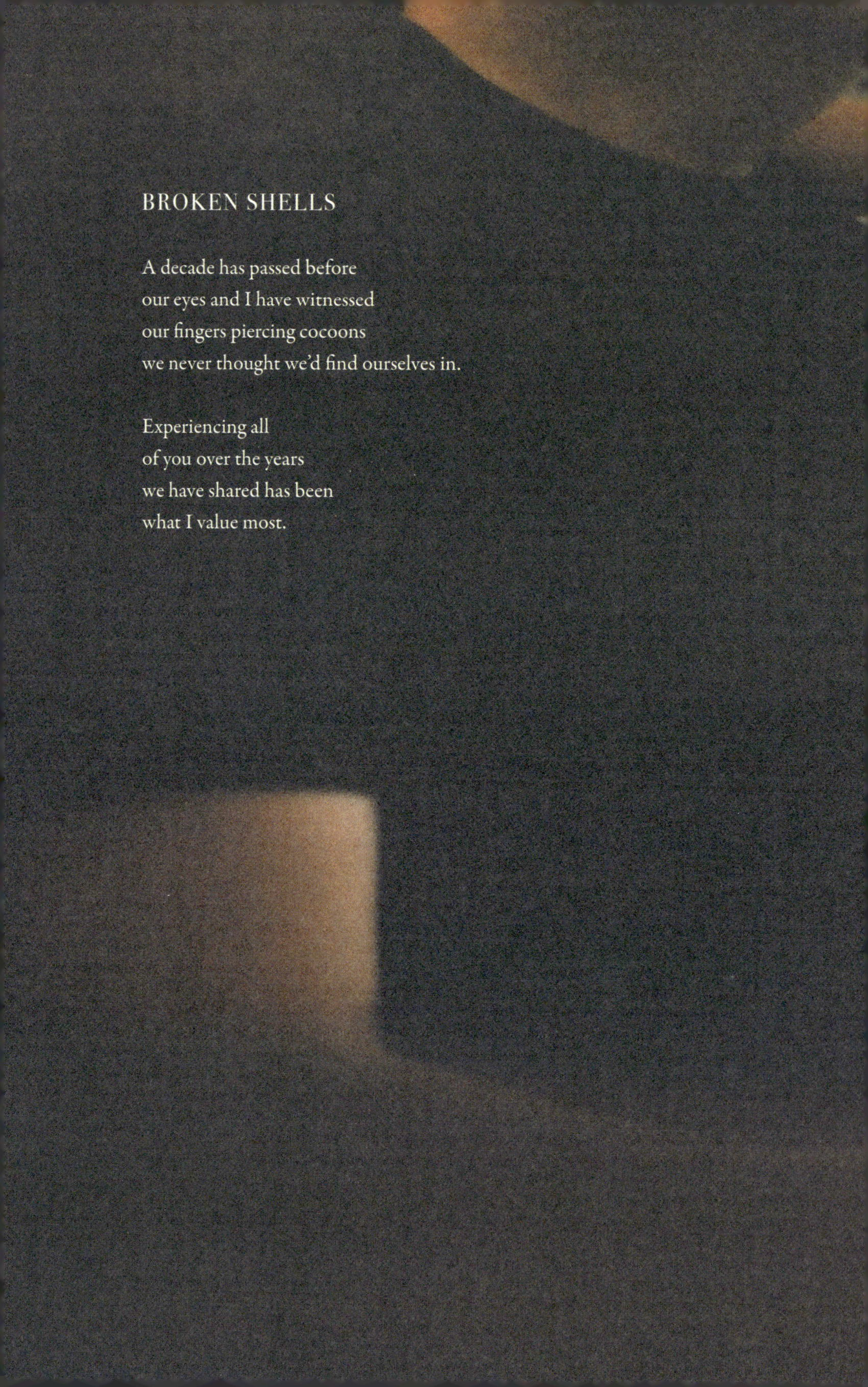

BROKEN SHELLS

A decade has passed before
our eyes and I have witnessed
our fingers piercing cocoons
we never thought we'd find ourselves in.

Experiencing all
of you over the years
we have shared has been
what I value most.

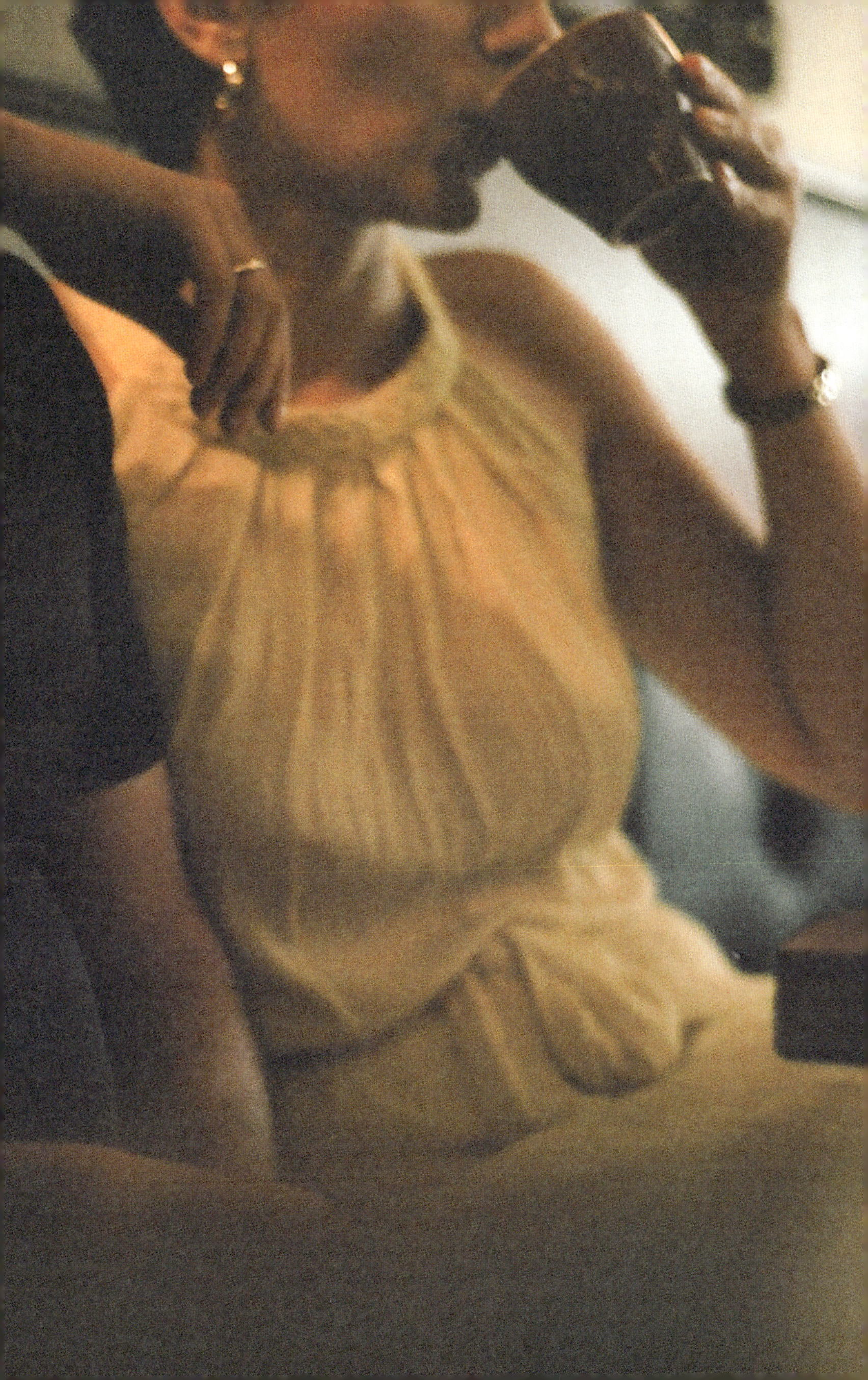

LIKE US

Two cats holding
one another on the neighbor's
patio as the rain quietly patters
over us. They're like us, you say.
Like us.

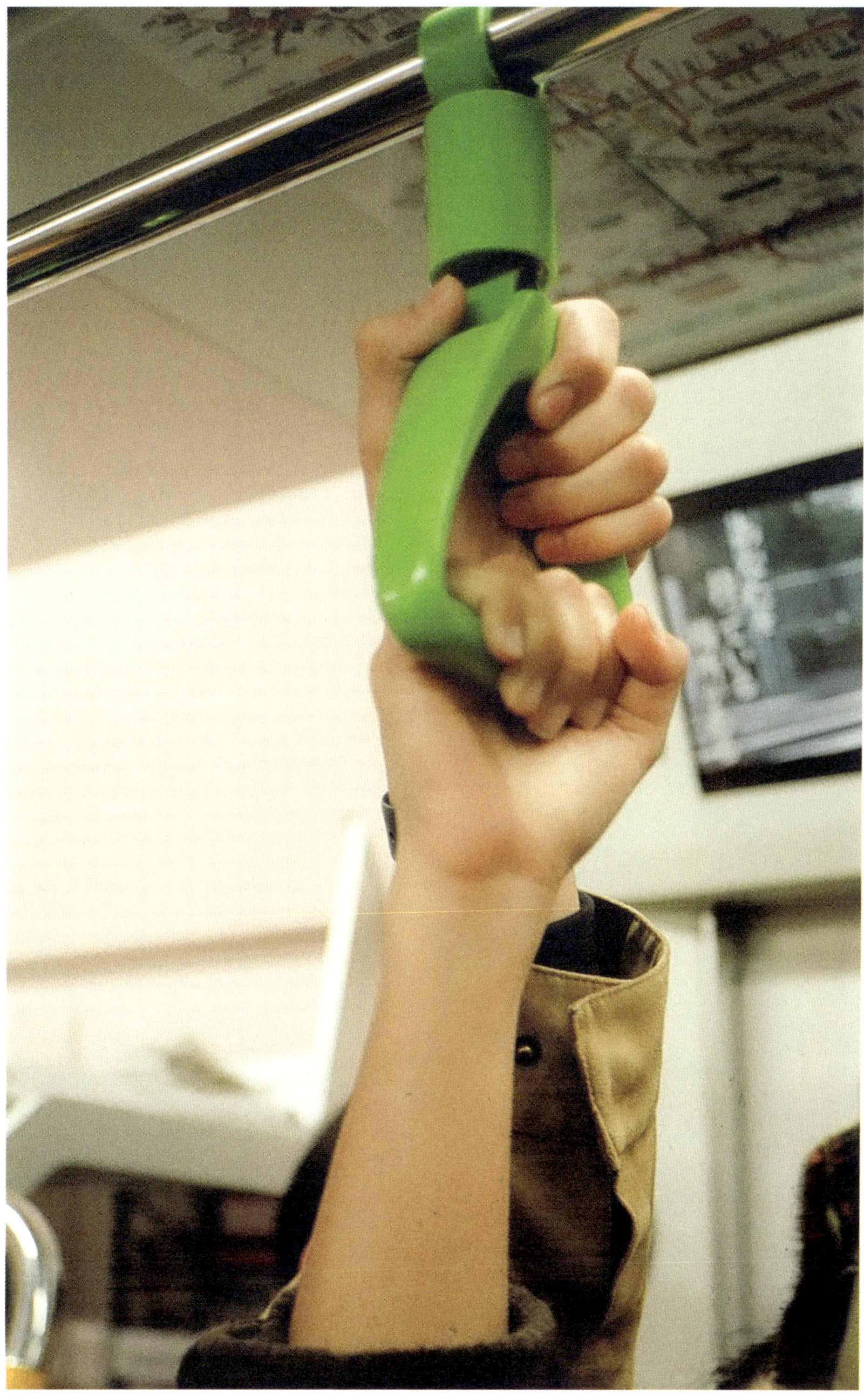

SCATTER ME

in the soil of the tree where
we first opened our lips for one another.
Go there when you ache for me.

I'll be an age when I adored you
like air itself. I will be there, awaiting you.

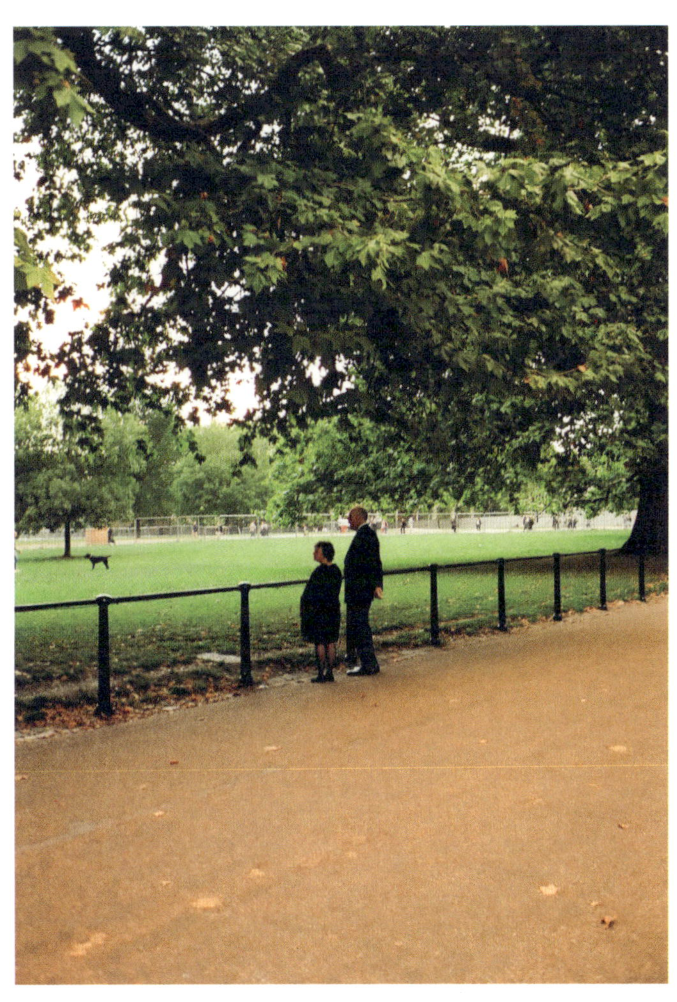

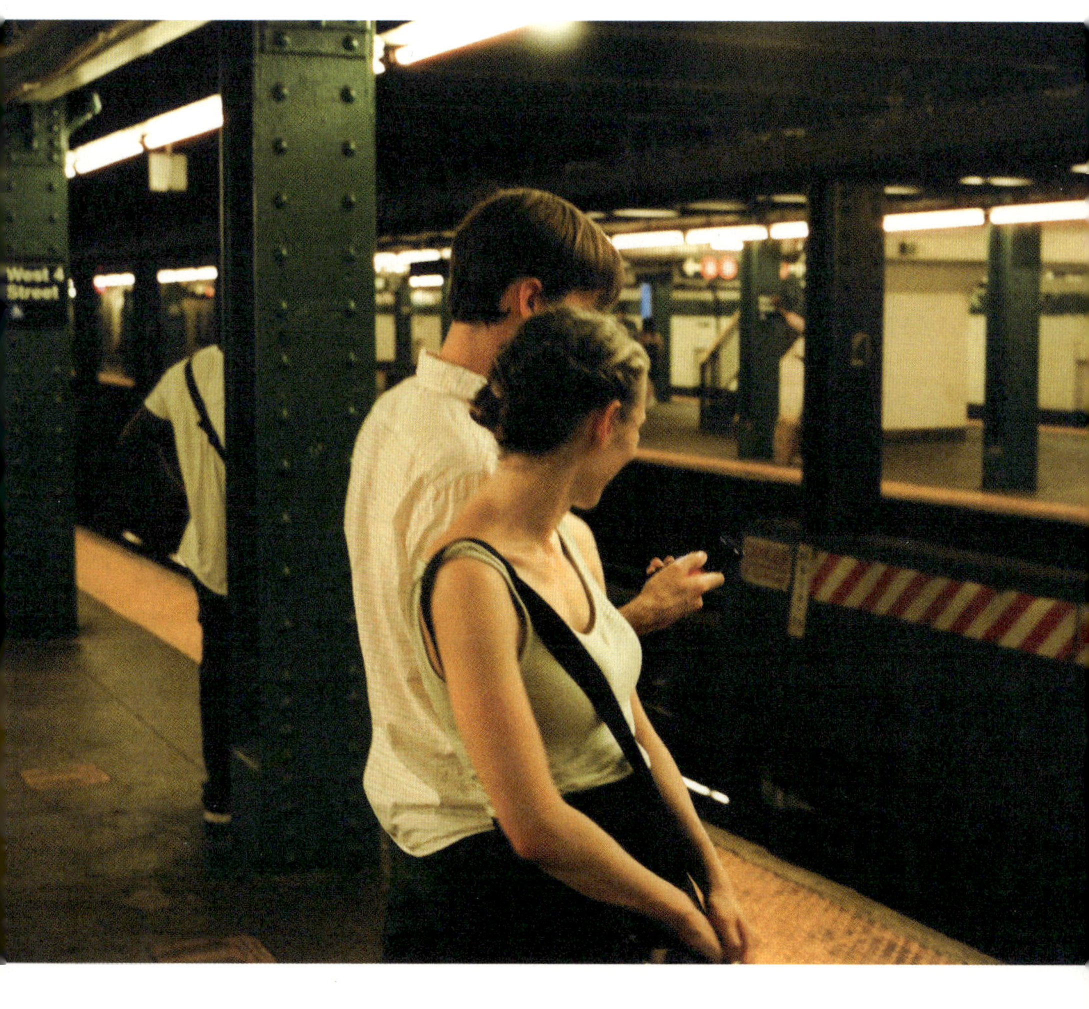
West 4
Street

MY CHILDHOOD

Of all the love
that has been lost, that never
had moments to breathe with me.
The sense of being adrift, able
to pinpoint the many ways
love was locked away from me, rumbling
against cages and me, begging.

In the days since, I still struggle
with accepting the light others talk
to me with. Unnatural in its many ways,
I slow time down so I can grow more and more,
to experience that which is distant to me.

THE PIT

When we leave one another, the pit
inside of me widens. A brown seed of
a peach to a lake, some may call it
an ocean. I know I must learn

how to find comfort in discomfort.
To hold close what resides in me.
For when I know its name,
the pit becomes easier

to swallow.

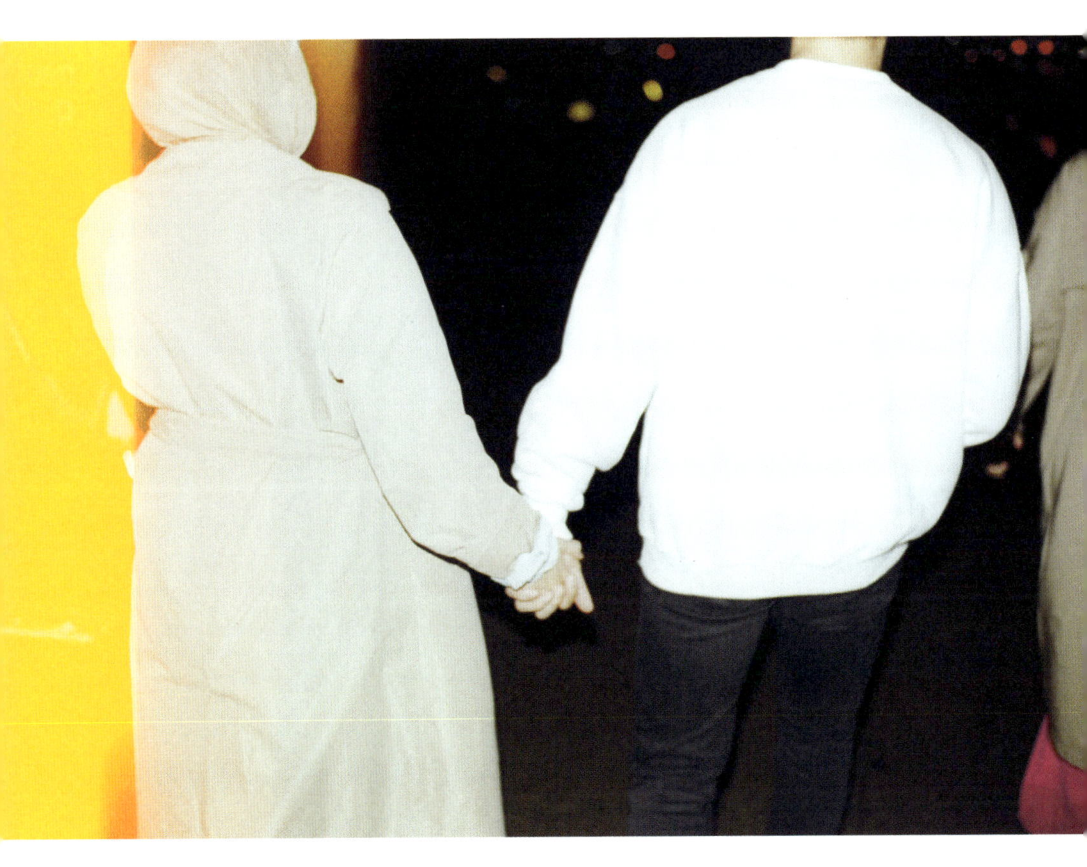

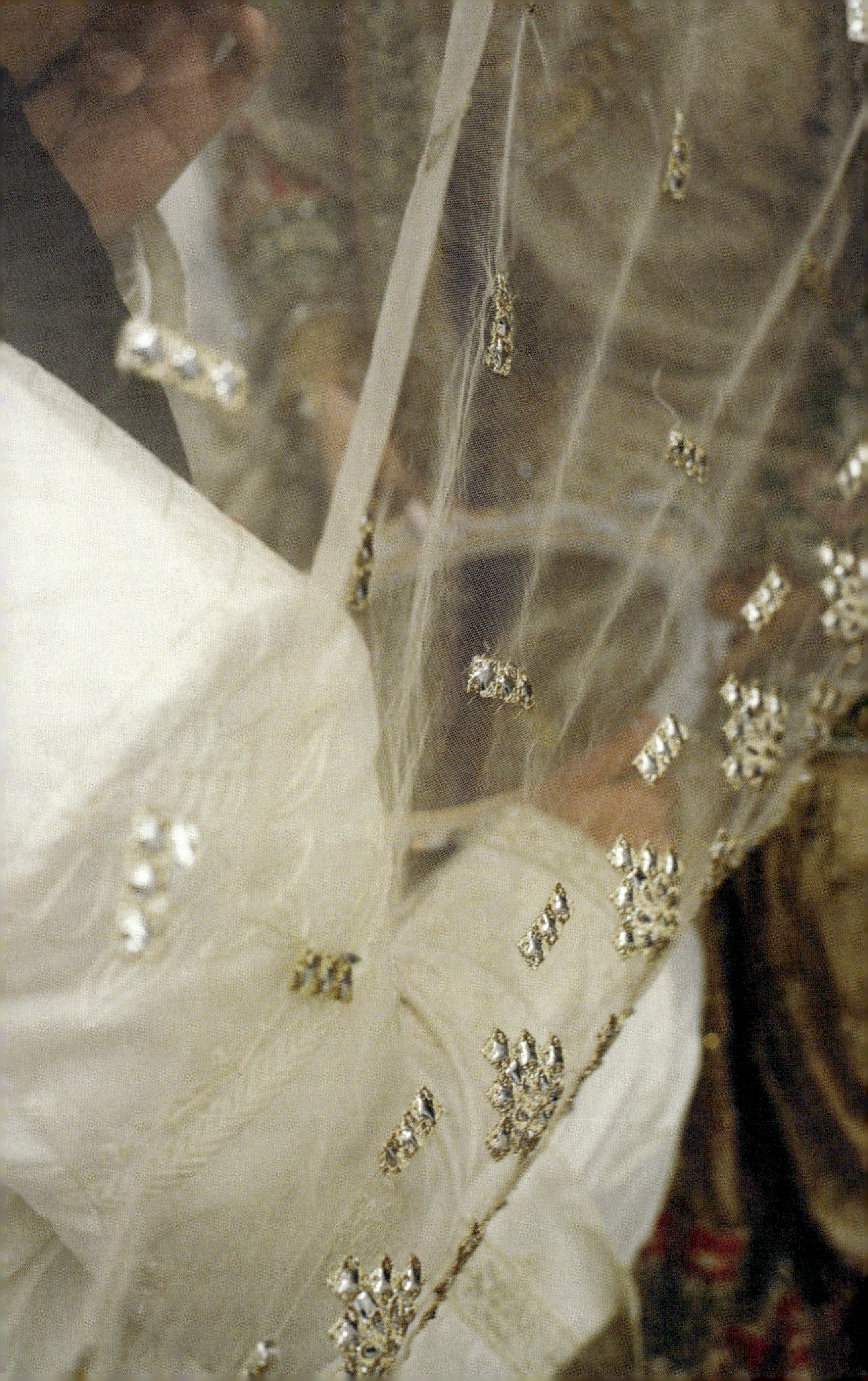

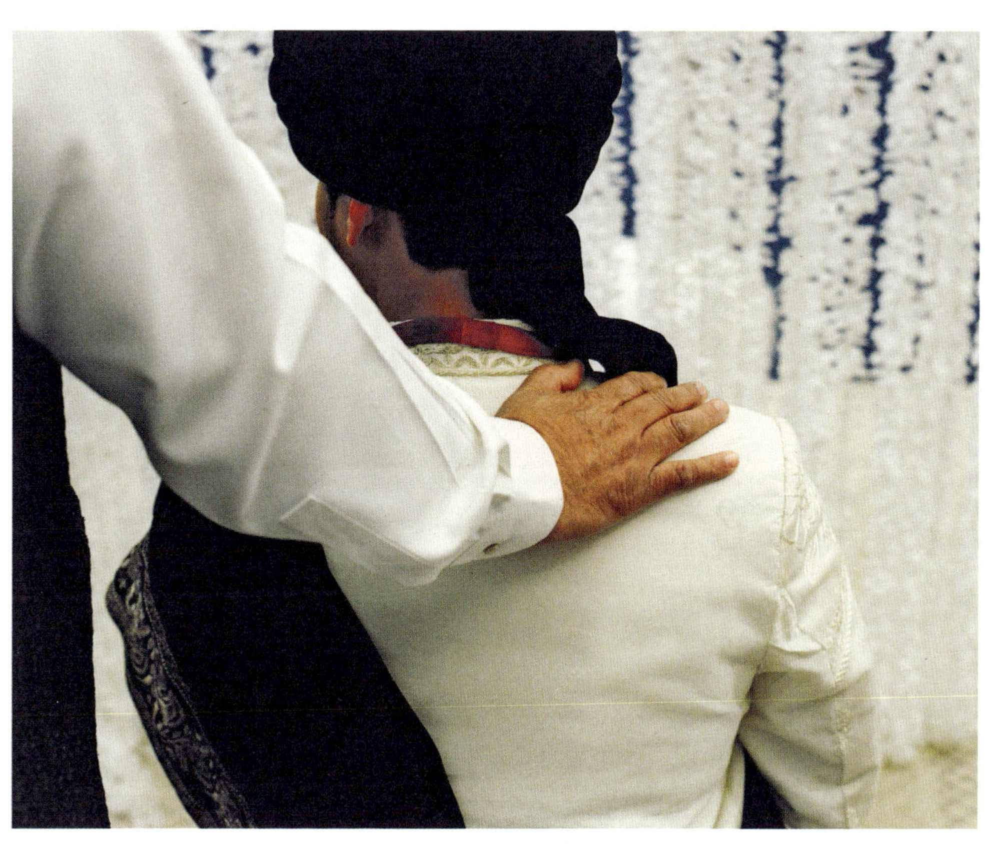

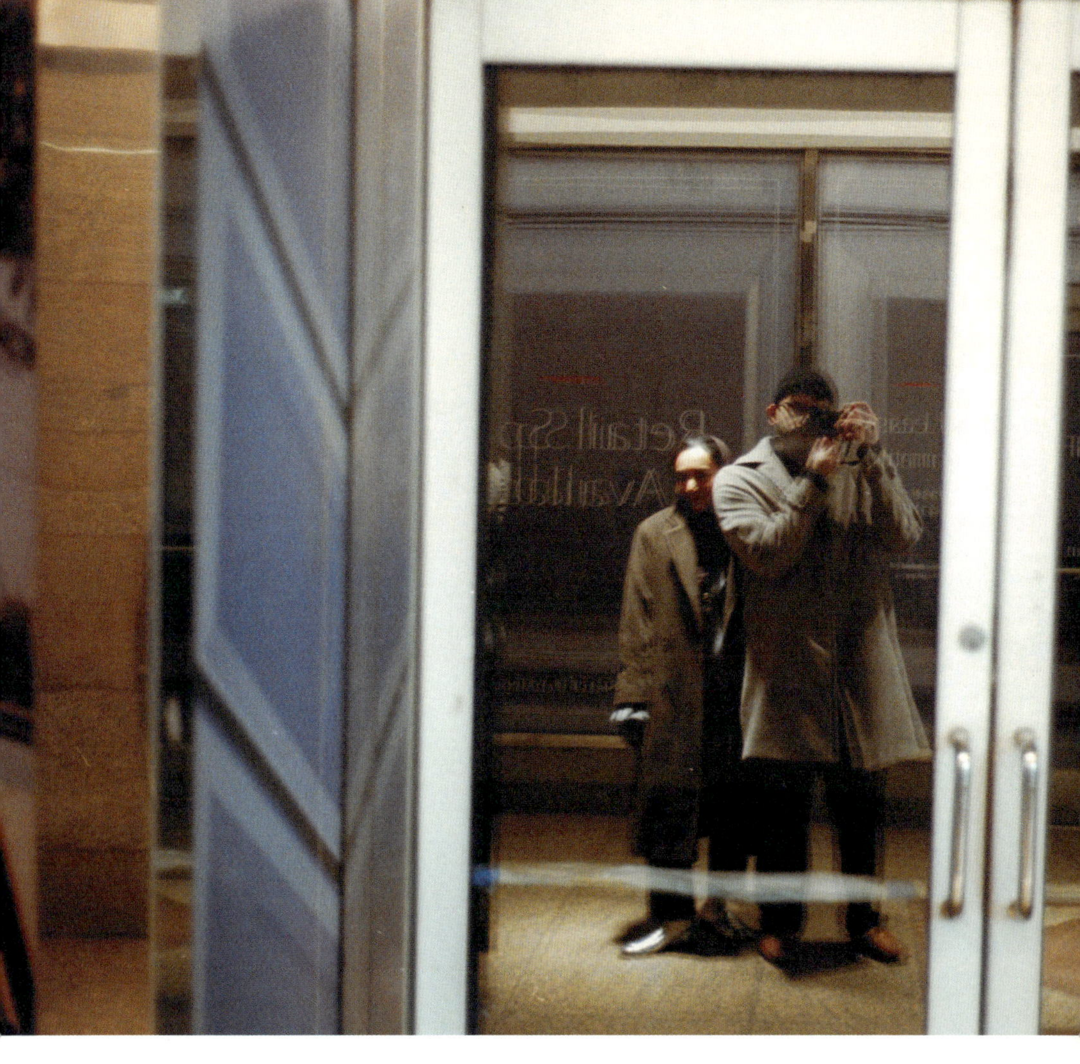

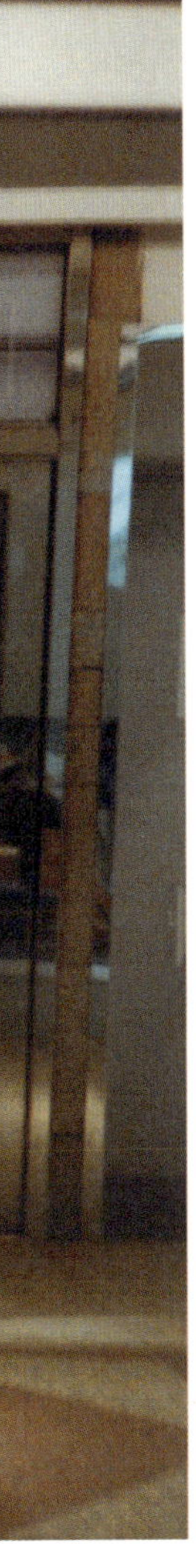

WE WILL REMAIN

In the simplicity of time
I am confronted with the fact that our skin
will never be

as vibrant as it once was. That all our years
we spent together are gone,
difficult to retrieve, as if there is a deep

hole in the ground, our arms
too short to reach and our nails
scraping the shell of a history

we buried. Panic
sets in, knowing I will never get
those moments back. Laying down

and staring at the glistening night sky,
I think of how our skin will wither more
and more and our hues will continue

to decay, leaving only our barren
essence, which stands larger than the shell
that carries them.

Because we are together,
and only with one another
can we remain.

REBIRTH FROM ASH

We play Spit on a little
table, eat warm pasta as the tiny cabin
fills with the smell of wood-fire burning

from outside the small window, its light hue flickering
across the pane. In quiet moments, you ask
me how in such a lively world we managed

to accept one another. I think of the matches
we held. Of how bright we were separately.
And together, even more.

Forced creation—rebirth.
The wood's flickering quiets,
ash cultivating into the soil below.

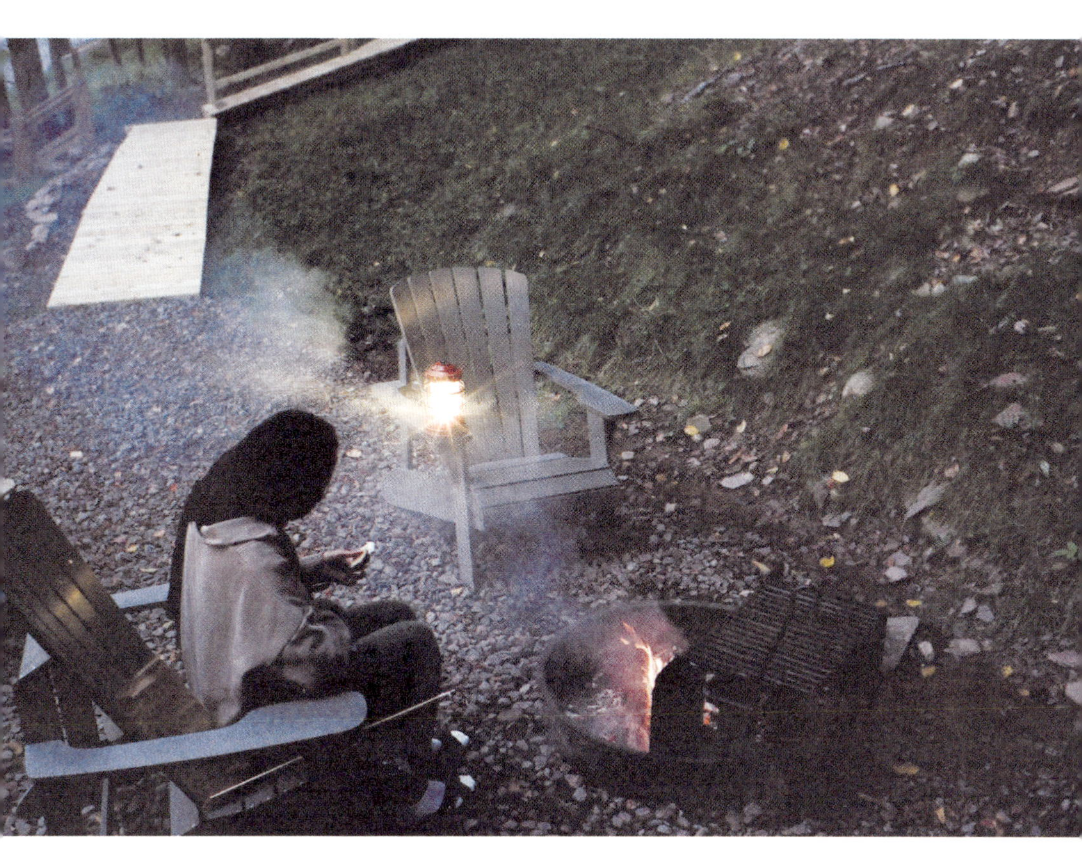

IN AN ABSOLUTE

destruction of myself, I become
darkness. I look up or down or

to my sides, and there's no difference.
My wrists are pained and my face

is wet—from sweat or tears I can't tell
these days. I don't want anyone

to hear me, to burden those who love
me more than I know myself.

Who love me despite my many
misgivings. Who love me even when I refuse

my own reflection. Looking back,
I need more than I desire myself.

Even when you hear me from outside
the darkened room, I give in.

UP TO ME, ONLY ME

You have brought me
happiness which doesn't exist elsewhere,
so much that I wonder how the dim crater
that lives within me still thumps against
my ribs, my filling shell. *Why are you still here,*
I ask, knowing full well only I am responsible
for its caring.

SPRING LAKE

You held me as the sand
enveloped my feet and I felt
the ocean's breeze. Smelled the salted

sea and fried potatoes
and sugared funnel cakes.
The seagulls cried as they circled above

us and I pulled a hair out
of my arm, unflinching, to make sure
this was real. I had been living

as if I was weightless, my life
not my life but
an onlooker—as if I was barred

in a theater. To feel what I see,
but not experience it fully.
I held the strand between

my thumb and finger,
tightening my grip before burying
it with the shells, brushing my fingers

over the granules. Cries
from above, as if we're being
spoken to.

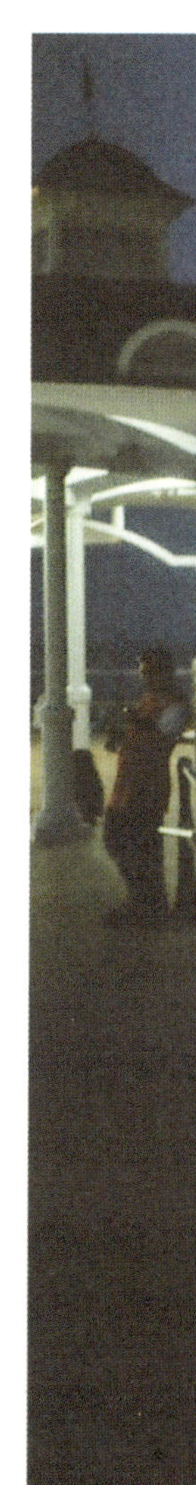

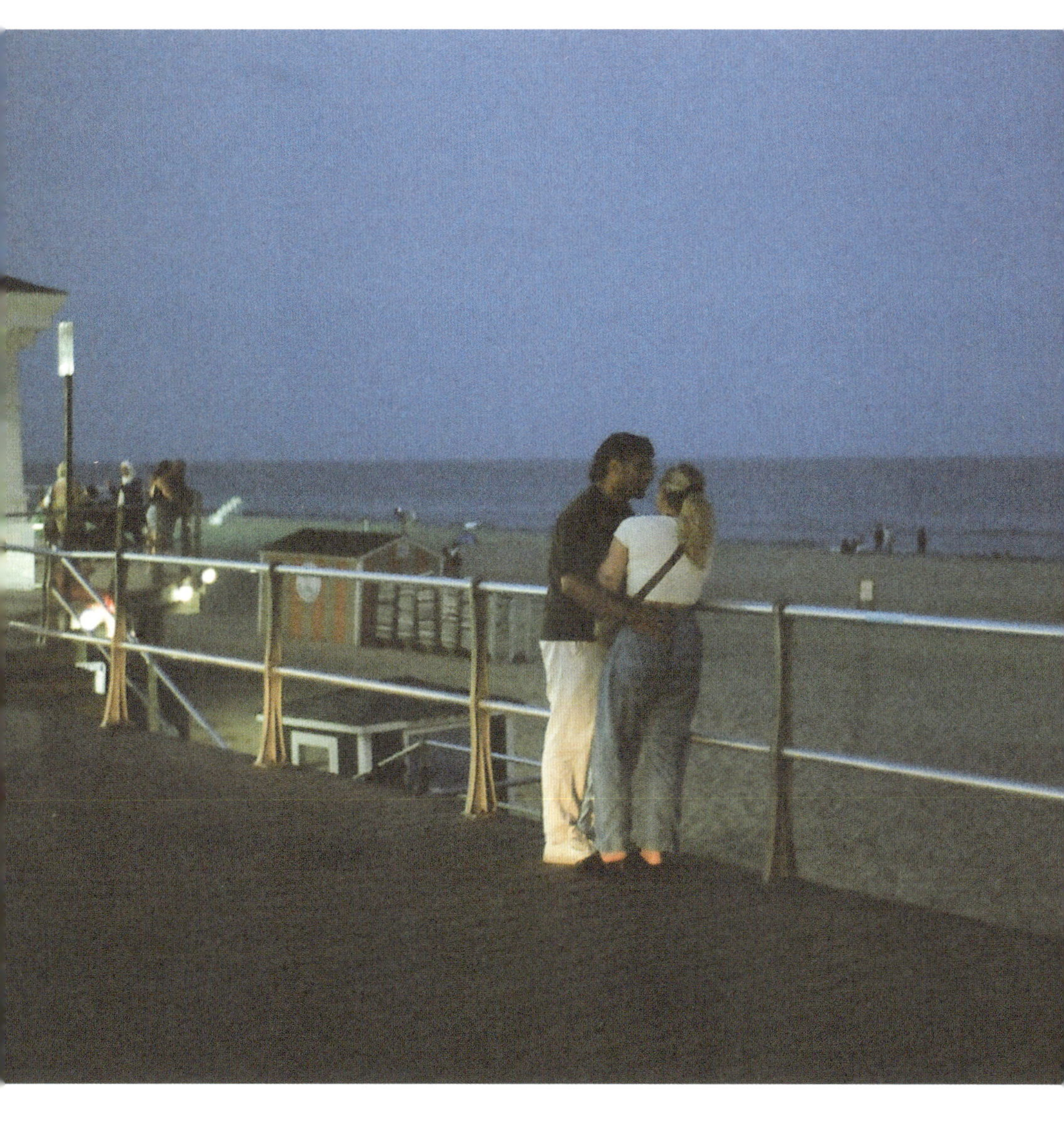

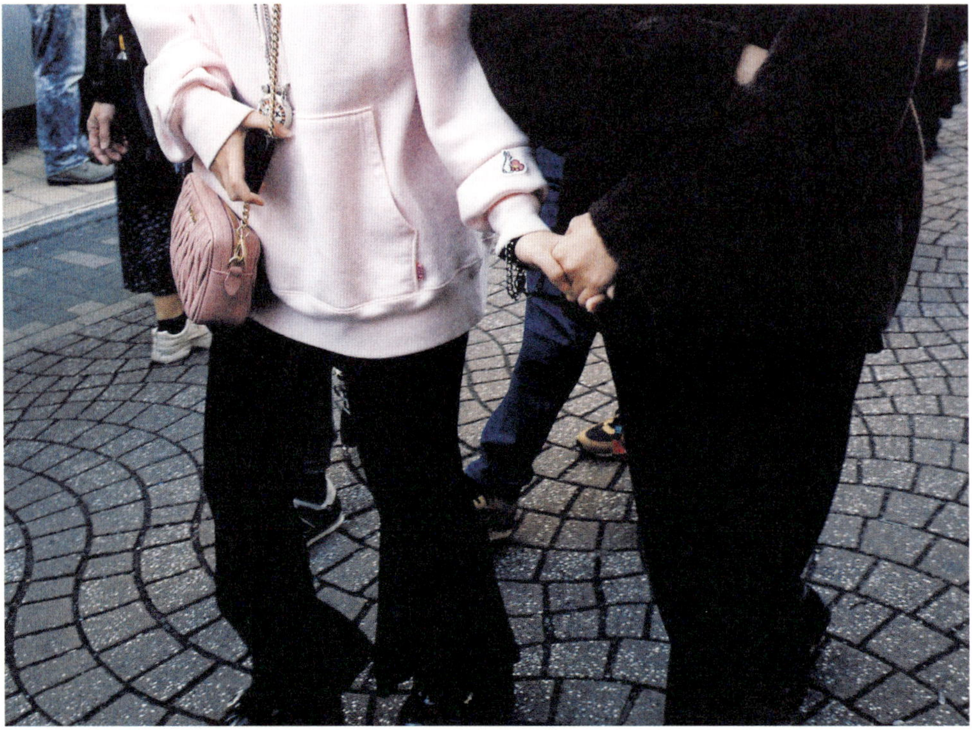

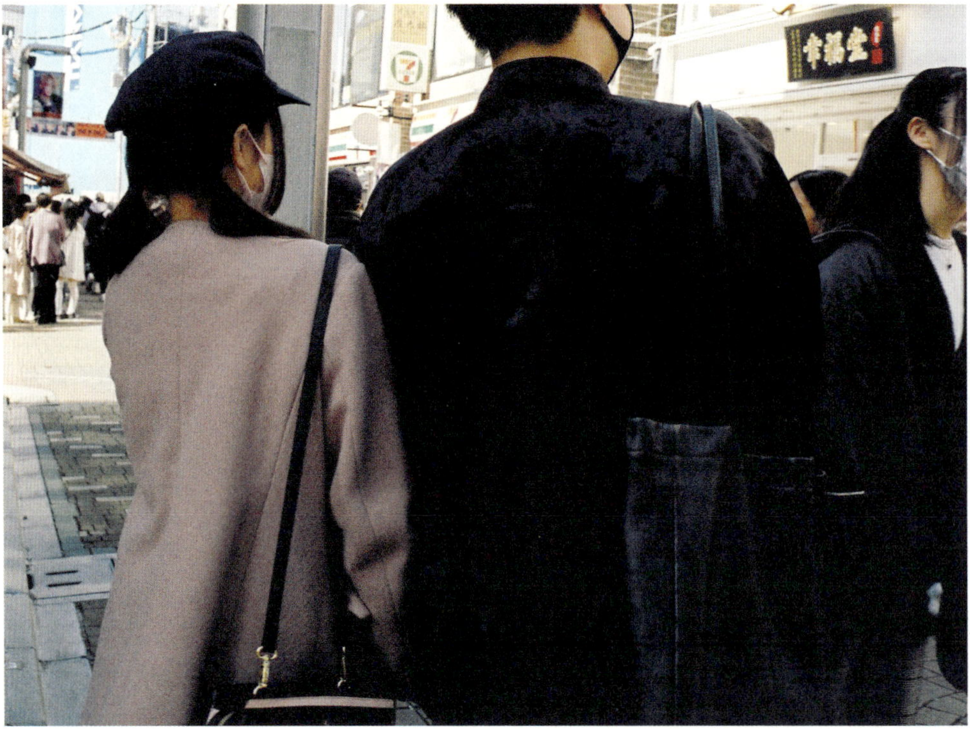

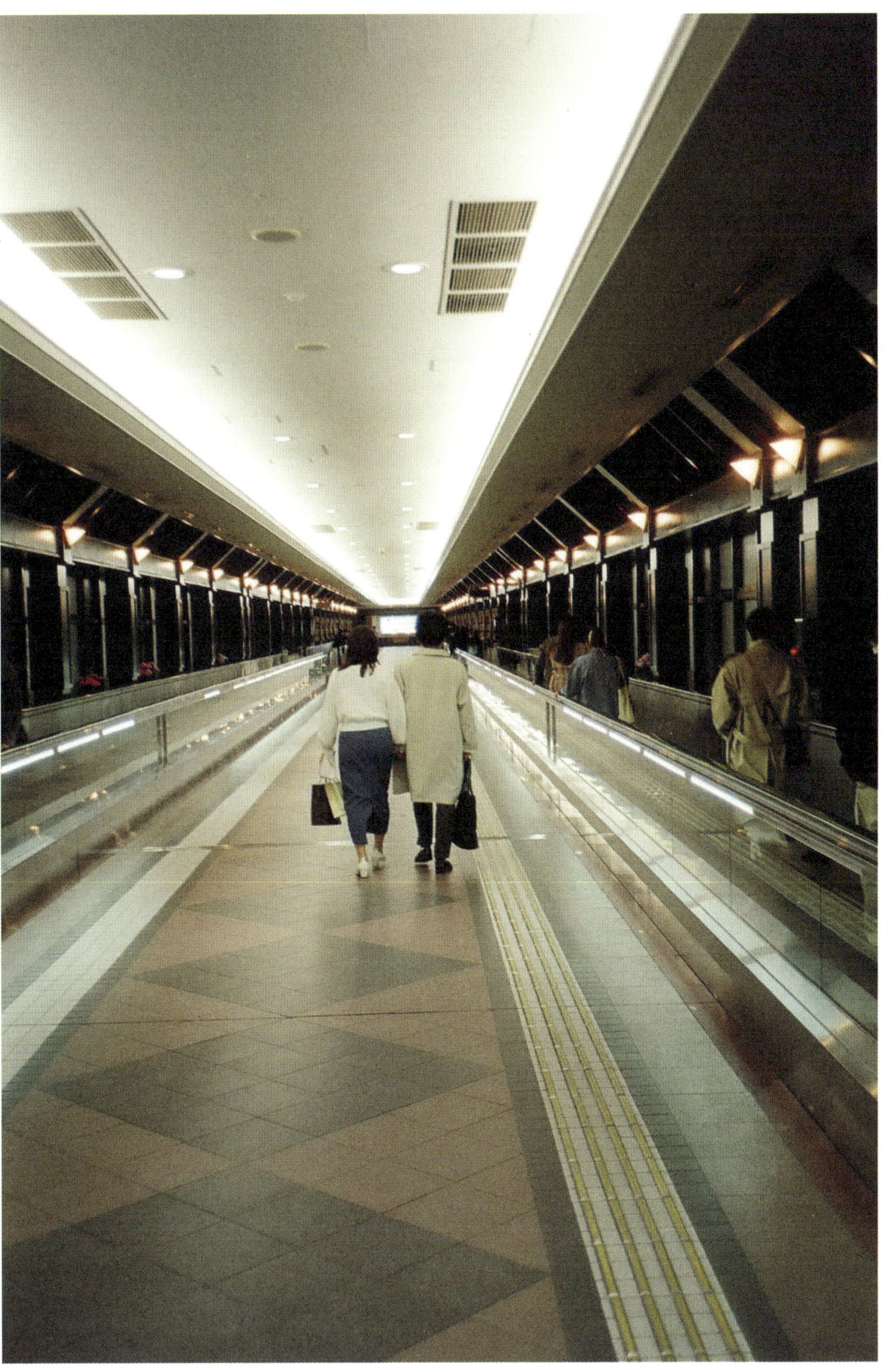

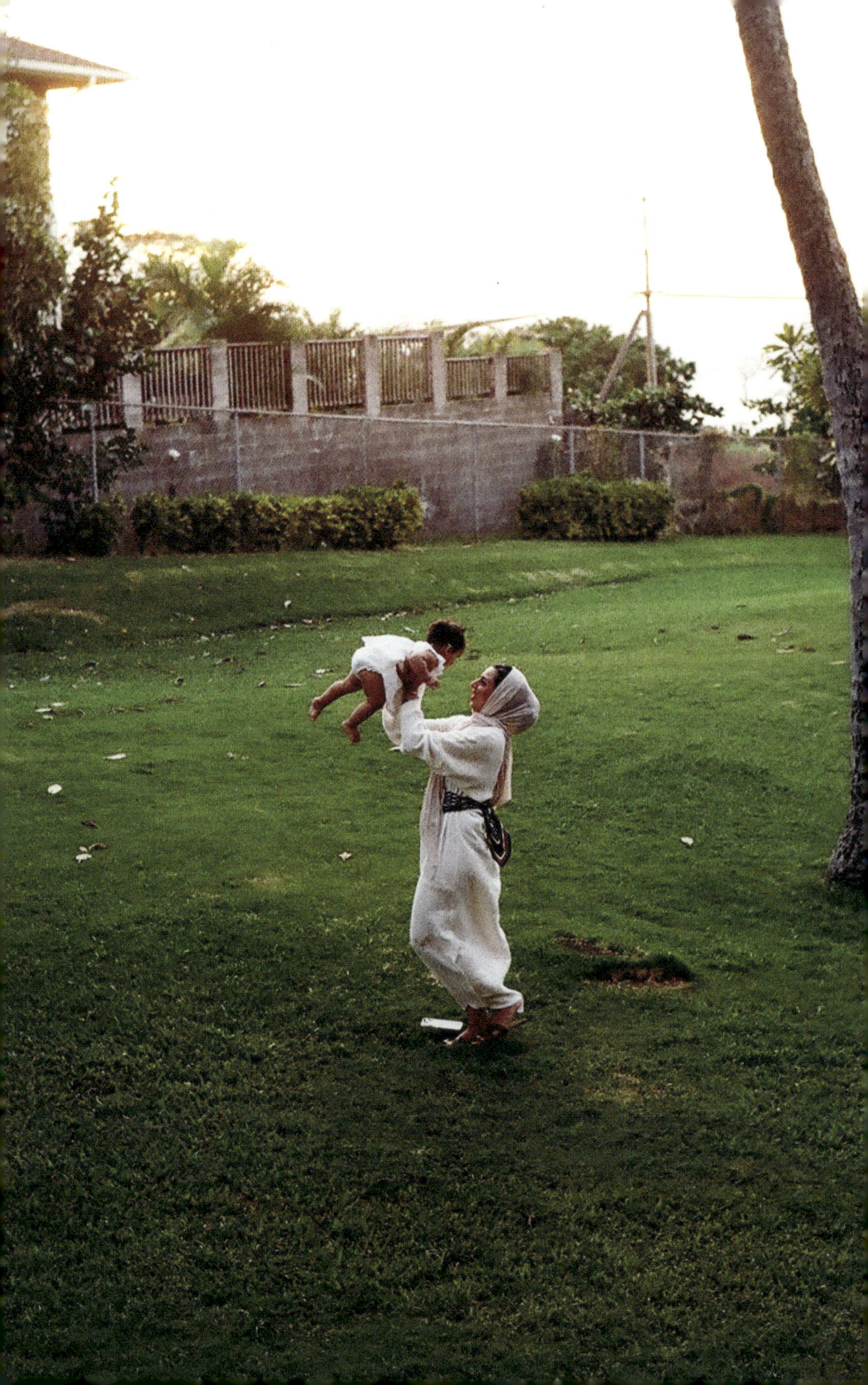

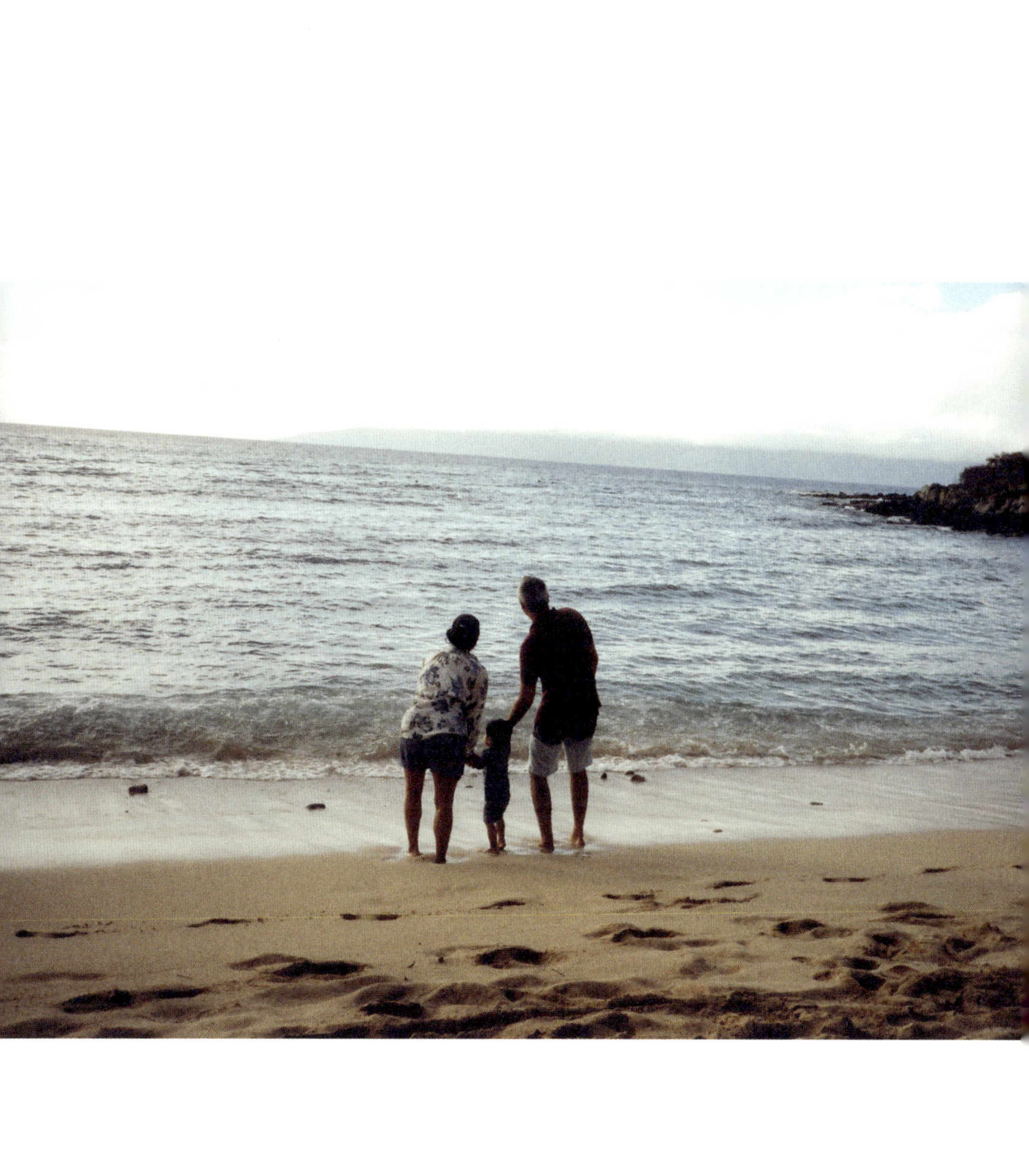

AN OATH

Each time I blink, I take
a snapshot of this moment.

Two silly roses sit in a bucket of water,
petals hanging off the sides.

You tell me about the ache that
lives in you for how life was once

full of passion, how easily
words would slip out of us,

putting us two in a love-
drunk stupor. Especially us,

palms on my cheek, especially us.
Small passions, the way I hold you tight,

wishing there was a space on our skin to lock
us in place. I blink, hoard another snapshot,

put it in the box under the bed like
my mother kept hers, dust resting on top.

You blink at me, and I hope
you also have your own box of memories

in a place I can't find. And know
that this is also a bare act of love.

TONES OF MY HISTORY

I look into the mirror and feel
my skin. Indents forming crow's feet,

knowing years have decayed and more
will, too. These days, I instill

little areas of my home for pondering.
In the kitchen while I'm cooking or sitting

at the bottom of the stairs, watching
the cats play. The way life carries difference

now compared to years prior. My first home, where
the screen door shut too hard and bugs sang

in lush foliage. The stray cats caring for
one another in the abandoned garage

and endearment surrounding me.
To my last home, where I saw devotions wither,

burned past the ground, as if it never had life or
no one wanted to think it ever did. Being forced

to look in the mirror then, notice
my skin—its colors leaving wetly

every way they could, as if I was not
worthy to house them. At the bottom

of the stairs or in the kitchen, those rotting
structures exist within me

still and yet, the door silently opens,
nature's chords greeting me.

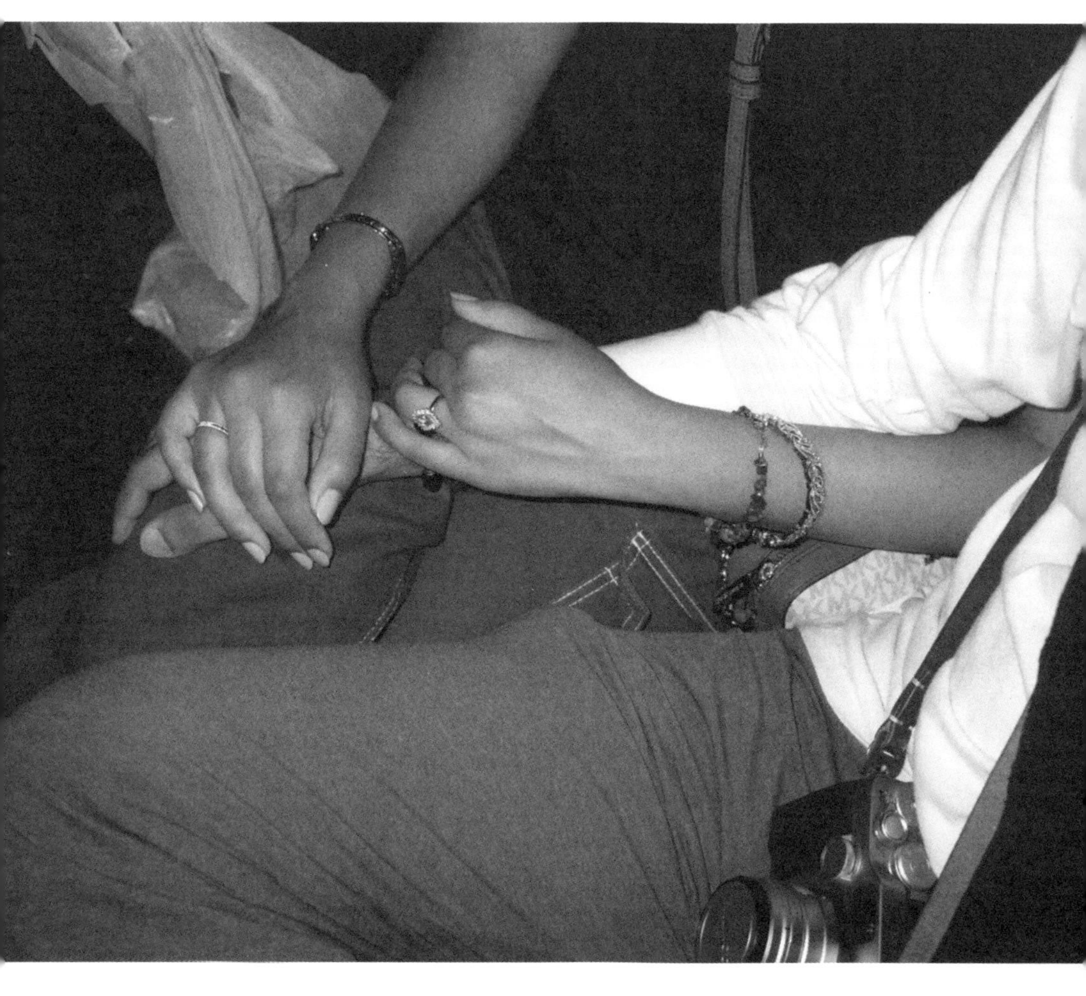

LATE AT NIGHT

You live many lives
as you dream peacefully,
ones I will never
experience with you.

I grow desirous of your slumber.

JUST KIDS

I look at you this morning as you're asleep and can't help but think of how young we used to be. We were just kids, not knowing how this life would unfold and how together we would be now. How we've grown to understand the complexities of our emotions, the sadness that latches onto me like a tick every day, and feel it more than I do. Tweezing it out whenever you spot it feeding off my body. And me knowing how to breathe in unison with you when you need it. How early on we felt as if we were on a faulty foundation, to towering over the years we have lived.

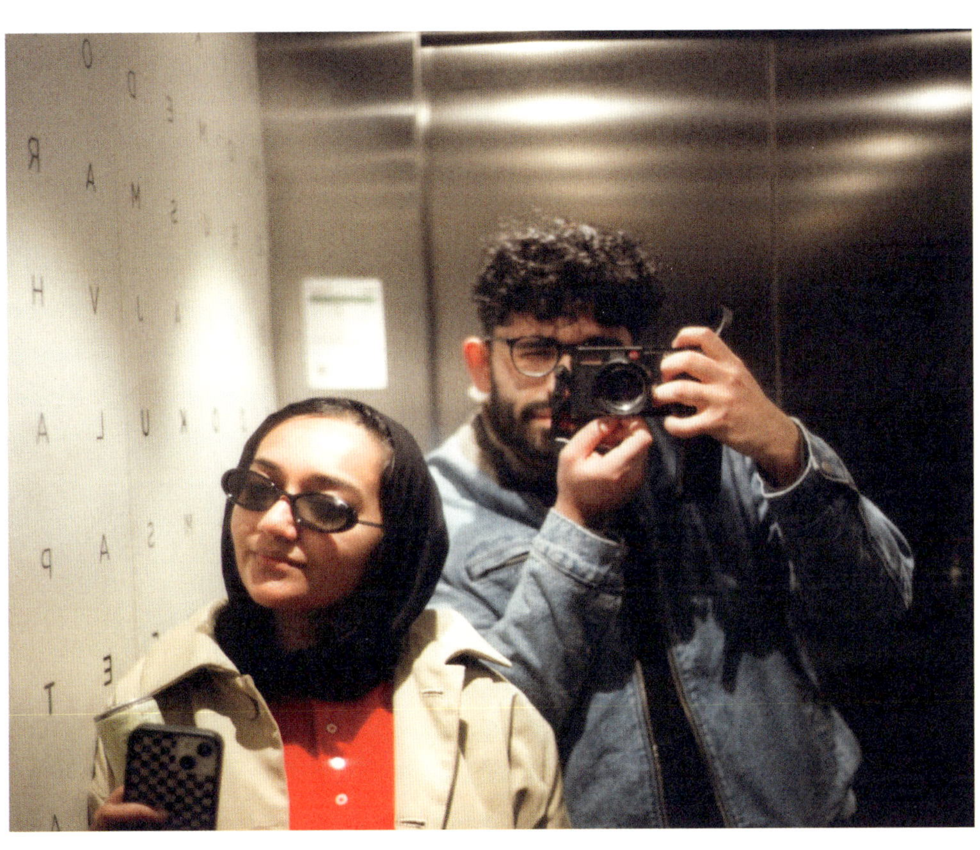

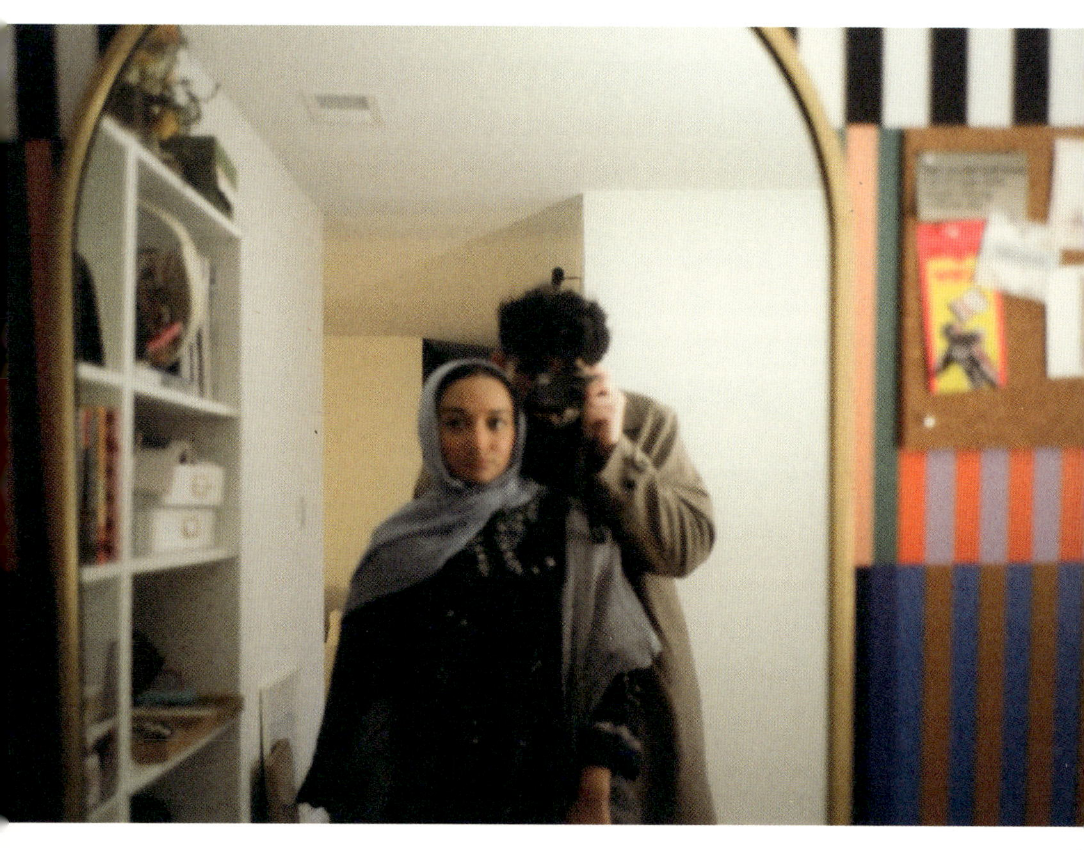

ACKNOWLEDGMENTS

First and foremost, I want to thank every reader who's picked up my books from the beginning. I wouldn't be anywhere without you. It's a surreal, and mostly odd, feeling, knowing that there are readers out there who have your books. It honestly doesn't feel real, but I'm trying to let it sink in more and more. Thank you, thank you, thank you.

Yusra, for always giving me reasons. To live, to write, to prosper. We met over a decade ago, and every year has been more of a blessing. Even in the years I've lost, I don't feel like I truly have only because you're still by my side. You've shown me how love is never linear—how you went from hating cats to owning two and even fostering cats any chance we get. Being with you is a trip, and I'm excited to see all the places we'll go. Without you and your inspiration, this book wouldn't exist.

Immense gratitude for my close friend, Imam. My world wouldn't be the same without you in my life. From board game nights to playing video games, being with you makes my heart full. Thank you for always holding me as close as I hold you.

To my family—Aqsa, Nida, Eiman, Mama, the kids. Thank you for being home when we were younger and altering that home as we got older. I hope for all of us to continue to age with each other—I'm excited to see what our futures will hold. I'm grateful I get to call you my family.

For Yusra's family—Taaha, Wisam, Hafsa, Sania, Shayan, Ammi, Abu, the kids. Thank you for always believing in my work, for being like a family I've always wanted in this life. Every ounce of love you give me never goes unnoticed.

To the person who shares my love of cameras and film: I'm grateful to Taaha for always going with me on photo walks and talking cameras with me.

I hold all those days close, when we used to walk around New York City and every new city we went to, taking pictures of everything we found interesting. I hope we can always do that; I hope we never lose interest in what surrounds us. Thank you for also scanning and working on this book with me. You're one of the best photographers I know, and the world will know that one day as well.

To every writer and artist who inspires and motivates me: Sarah Mokh, Madisen Kuhn, Jennah Janouk, Faye Wikner, Chris Salerno, Sara Bawany, and Mashnun Munir. You all keep me going in so many different ways, and I want to be a better writer for all of you, to make you all proud of the work I create.

And a final thanks to Andrews McMeel Publishing for giving *Notes on Love* a home. This is a project I've looked forward to making, and I'm so happy it gets to be with Danys and everyone over at AMU.

Thank you again for reading. I really hope you enjoyed *Notes on Love* and continue to stick around. I'm so happy you're here.

With love,
FSY